W9-BVH-042

Games for Language Learning
New Edition

CAMBRIDGE HANDBOOKS FOR LANGUAGE TEACHERS

General Editor: Michael Swan

This is a series of practical guides for teachers of English and other languages. Illustrative examples are usually drawn from the field of English as a foreign or second language, but the ideas and techniques described can equally well be used in the teaching of any language.

In this series:

Games for Language Learning

NEW EDITION

Andrew Wright
David Betteridge and
Michael Buckby

CAMBRIDGE
UNIVERSITY PRESS

Published by the Press Syndicate of the University of Cambridge
The Pitt Building, Trumpington Street, Cambridge CB2 1RP
40 West 20th Street, New York, NY 10011–4211, USA
10 Stamford Road, Oakleigh, Victoria 3166, Australia

© Cambridge University Press 1983

First published 1979
Fourth printing 1982
Second edition 1984
Eleventh printing 1992

Printed in Great Britain at
the University Press, Cambridge

Library of Congress catalogue card no: 83–20862

British Library cataloguing in publication data
Wright, Andrew, 1937–
Games for language learning. – 2nd ed.
(Cambridge handbooks for language teachers)
1. English language – Study and teaching
– Foreign students   2. Educational
games
I. Title   II. Betteridge, David   III. Buckby,
Michael
428.2′4′0768   PE1128

ISBN 0 521 25861 8 hardback
ISBN 0 521 27737 X paperback

Copyright
the law allows a reader to make a single copy of part of a book
for purposes of private study. It does not allow the copying of
entire books or the making of multiple copies of extracts. Written
permission for any such copying must always be obtained from
the publisher in advance.

SE

Contents

87242

Acknowledgements

We should like to acknowledge our debt to Donn Byrne, Jim Kerr, Alan Maley, Mario Rinvolucri, and the British Council, English Language Teaching Institute, London.

Drawings by Andrew Wright.

Preface to the new edition

. . . and a thank you to the many teachers with whom we have worked.

We have worked with teachers from many countries since the first edition of *Games for Language Learning* was published. We have discussed with the teachers their experience of using the book. Their very positive feelings have been encouraging to us. Equally valuable have been their perceptive observations and practical suggestions for improvement. At the same time we have continued to collect, adapt and devise games. We are delighted, therefore, to have the opportunity to produce a new and enlarged edition.

In this new edition we have:
– added new sections
– added more than 100 new games and variations
– added a description of the character of each family of games in order to help teachers to develop their own variations
– modified the index.

Introduction

Games in language learning

Why games?

Language learning is hard work. One must make an effort to
understand, to repeat accurately, to manipulate newly understood
language and to use the whole range of known language in conversation
or written composition. Effort is required at every moment and must be
maintained over a long period of time. Games help and encourage many
learners to sustain their interest and work.

Games also help the teacher to create contexts in which the language
is useful and meaningful. The learners *want* to take part and in order to
do so must understand what others are saying or have written, and they
must speak or write in order to express their own point of view or give
information.

Many games cause as much density of practice as more conventional
drill exercises; some do not. What matters, however, is the *quality* of
practice.

The contribution of drilling lies in the concentration on a language
form and its frequent use during a limited period of time. Many games
provide this repeated use of a language form. By making the language
convey information and opinion, games provide the key feature of 'drill'
with the opportunity to sense the working of language as living
communication.

The need for meaningfulness in language learning has been accepted
for some years. A useful interpretation of 'meaningfulness' is that the
learners respond to the content in a definite way. If they are amused,
angered, challenged, intrigued or surprised the content is clearly
meaningful to them. Thus the meaning of the language they listen to,
read, speak and write will be more vividly experienced and, therefore,
better remembered.

If it is accepted that games can provide intense and meaningful
practice of language, then they must be regarded as *central* to a
teacher's repertoire. They are thus not for use solely on wet days and at
the end of term!

Games can be found to give practice in all the skills (reading, writing,
listening and speaking), in all the stages of the teaching/learning

sequence (presentation, repetition, recombination and free use of language) and for many types of communication (e.g. encouraging, criticising, agreeing, explaining).

Information gap and opinion gap

The terms 'information gap' and 'opinion gap' are now widely used to describe features essential to so much communication in our daily lives. We speak or write because we want to pass on information or convey an opinion which we think the receiver might be interested in. If the receiver is familiar with the information and is of the same opinion, there is no gap and he/she will probably switch off. It may seem terribly obvious! But in much foreign-language learning there is no information gap at all and opinions are rarely asked for. The teacher usually asks a question which the learner knows the teacher can answer! The teacher is more interested in the form than in the content of what the learner says.

An understanding of the principle of information gap and opinion gap, and a belief that they should be intrinsic to most language-learning activities is essential for any teacher using the games in this book.

The following is an example of one of the best known of the information gap games.

Describe and draw a picture: One person has a picture and does not show it to his/her partner. There is thus an information gap. The first learner then tries to describe the picture so that the second learner can draw it. Language is used to bridge the gap. The picture drawn by the second learner is then visible evidence of whether the gap has been closed.

Who are games for?

Enjoyment of games is not restricted by age. Some individuals, regardless of age, may be less fond of games than others. But so much depends on the appropriateness of the games and the role of the player.

It is generally accepted that young learners and adults are very willing to play games. (This partly depends on the learners' socio-cultural background.) Early teenagers tend to be more self-conscious and one must take into account their reticence when selecting games for them. Games which can be played in pairs or groups may be particularly useful in this case. It is clear to all observers of classroom practice that the teacher's own belief in the usefulness and appropriateness of a game affects the learners' response. We have observed games and materials normally used in primary schools being accepted by businessmen owing to the conviction of the teacher!

We have already acknowledged that teenage learners might be reluctant to play games. We also acknowledge that many people are so anxious to learn English in order to pass examinations or to improve their employment prospects that they look on games as unnecessary. If you have such committed learners you must clearly respect their point of view and be able to justify the use of each game in terms of the density and meaningfulness of practice it provides.

Many of the games in this book can, with minor adaptations, be used by beginners, intermediate and advanced students. However, some of the variations described are for specific levels of ability and achievement.

It is important to note that the most advanced and dedicated students can enjoy and value games if the content and language used are relevant to them.

It follows from the above that the real questions are not, 'Which age groups are games for?' or 'Which level?' but are much more specific:

1 Will the game take you a long time to prepare, compared with the amount of useful work you will get from it?
2 Will it be relatively easy for you to organise in the classroom?
3 Is it likely to interest the particular group of learners you have in mind?
4 Is the language or is the language skill you are concerned to teach intrinsic to the activity? Or are you (honestly!) just forcing it into the game?
5 Is the amount of language and the type of use enough to justify the use of the game? Or do you have another good reason for introducing it?

If your answer is 'yes' to each of these questions, then the game you have in mind is a highly efficient means of satisfying your learners' needs.

The spirit of real games

Our aim has been to find games which the learners would enjoy playing in their out-of-classroom lives. Of course, experience of teaching foreign languages shows that many learners *are* prepared to take part in games and activities which they would consider a little juvenile or rather boring in the mother tongue. However, there is a limit to learners' goodwill and we should not stray far from the aim of introducing games worth playing in their own right. It is often the activity expected of a learner which makes it into an acceptable game, or, on the other hand, into a mechanical exercise. One example of this must suffice.

The teacher places a number of pens, pencils, etc. in various places on the desk and asks a learner, for example, 'Where is the red pen?' As the red pen is obviously on the book, the learner *understands* the question as, 'What sentence in English describes the position of the pen?'

However, suppose the teacher says, 'Look carefully at the pens, pencils, etc. Now turn round. Where's the red pen? Can you remember?' In this case the learner's powers of memory are challenged and he/she is motivated to think and speak. And, most importantly, he/she is more likely to understand the question in a similar way to a native speaker.

The essential ingredient of a game is challenge. We do not believe that challenge is synonymous with competition. We are very happy to have compiled a book of games which do not, in most cases, rely on competition for their success. Indeed, we like the idea that many of the games depend on cooperation in accepting problems and searching for solutions to them. If this second edition continues to prove useful in promoting language learning and, at the same time, contributing in a small way to a belief in cooperation in the classroom, we shall be doubly pleased.

How to use this book

Index and grouping of games

The index (pp. 207–210) will help you find the game you need. The index is divided into two parts:

Structures (adjectives, negatives, possessives, tenses, etc.)
Types of communication (asking questions, giving reasons, comparing, correcting, etc.)

In the body of the book the games are grouped according to their general character and spirit (True/false games, Guessing and speculating games, Memory games, etc.). This grouping makes it clear that there are many different versions of each general type of game and that each version may give rise to different language and skills and be appropriate for different levels of language achievement.

Control

In this book we distinguish a range of language activities, from *controlled*, through an intermediate stage that we may call *guided*, to *free*. Control is greatest in teacher-led class or team games, especially those entailing listening or repeating; it is least in interaction games played by groups or pairs of learners on their own. In guided activities, some of the language that is required is provided by the teacher or by the content, while the rest of the language is provided by the learners themselves. In free activities, all the language is provided by the learners.

Class, individual, pair and group work

The notes on each game suggest which form of class organisation is appropriate. Of the four types of grouping, pair and group work are very important if each learner is to have sufficient oral practice in the use of the language. In class work it is easy to demonstrate that learners say only one or two sentences in a lesson or, indeed, in a week. The greatest 'mistake' (if oral ability is an aim) is for the learner not to speak at all! Thus, although some mistakes of grammar or pronunciation or idiom may be made in pair or group work, the price is worth paying. If the learners are clear about what they have to do and the language is not beyond them, there need be few mistakes.

Pair work: This is easy and fast to organise. It provides opportunities for intensive listening and speaking practice. Pair work is better than group work if there are discipline problems. Indeed, for all these reasons we often prefer to organise games in pair or general class work, rather than in group work.

Group work: Some games *require* four to six players; in these cases group work is essential. Membership of groups should be constant for the sake of goodwill and efficiency. If there is to be challenge between groups, they should be of mixed ability. If there is to be no such challenge, the teacher might choose groups according to ability: this is very much a personal choice. Many teachers consider it advisable to have a group leader. However, once more, it is our experience that groups can operate perfectly well without a group leader. The leader would normally be one of the more able learners. However, there is much to be said for encouraging a reticent learner by giving the responsibility to him/her. The leader's role is to ensure that the game or activity is properly organised and to act as an intermediary between learners and teacher.

The teacher's role, once the groups are in action, is to go from group to group listening in, contributing and, *if necessary*, correcting.

If you have not organised group work before, then it is advisable to work slowly towards it. First of all, make the learners familiar with work in pairs. Add to this games in which rows of learners (if that is how they are seated) play against you or between themselves. Finally, after perhaps several weeks, ask the rows of learners to group themselves together to play a game between themselves.

5

It is absolutely essential that the learners are totally familiar with the games they are asked to play. (It is helpful if they are familiar with the game in their own language.)

Once the learners are familiar with group work, new games are normally introduced in the following way:
– explanation by the teacher to the class
– demonstration of parts of the game by the teacher and one or two learners
– trial by a group in front of the class
– any key language and/or instructions written on the board
– first try by groups
– key language, etc. removed from the board.

Five practical points

If the teacher is unfamiliar with the use of language-teaching games then it is advisable to introduce them slowly as supplementary activities to whatever course book is used. Once the teacher is familiar with a variety of games, they can be used as a substitute for parts of the course which the teacher judges to be unsuitable. This book is a resource for the teacher, however, not a course in itself!

It is essential to choose games which are appropriate to the class in terms of language and type of participation. Having chosen an appropriate game, its character and the aims and rules must be made clear to the learners. It may be necessary to use the mother tongue to do this. If the learners are unclear about what they have to do, chaos and disillusionment may result.

Many teachers believe that competition should be avoided. It is possible to play the majority of games in this book with a spirit of challenge to achieve, rather than to 'do someone else down'. We believe that it is wrong and counter-productive to match learners of unequal ability even within a single exchange or challenge. The less able learner may 'give up' and the more able develop a false sense of his/her own achievement. We also believe it is wrong to compel an individual to participate. For many such learners there will be a point of 'readiness' to participate similar to the state of 'reading readiness' in young children. Learners reluctant to participate might be asked to act as judge and scorers.

As with all events in the classroom, it is advisable to stop a game and change to something else before the learners become tired of it. In this way their goodwill and concentration are retained.

We believe the teacher should never interrupt a game which is flowing successfully in order to correct a mistake in language use. It would suggest that the teacher is more concerned with form than with the exchange of ideas. In general, we think it better for the teacher to note the error and to comment on it later.

Collecting new games

Any games or activities which involve language and which your learners enjoy are language-learning material. You can find 'new' games by studying magazines, newspapers, radio and television programmes, party games and indeed by asking your learners. If you can create these games in the classroom and the language is appropriate, then they are useful.

It is usually difficult to find a new game for specific language practice just when you need it. It is a wise precaution to collect and file games for use whenever you happen to come across them. Games without materials can be described as in this book and filed in a ring binder. Games with visual materials could be kept in similar-sized envelopes bound in the same folder. It is helpful if the description of the game is written on the outside of the envelope and the visuals and handouts kept inside.

When collecting games it is important to note what language need only be understood by the players and what language must be used by them. (Indeed, in some games the learners are only expected to listen, understand, and, for example, point to a picture or carry out an action.) Thus, the language level is determined by the type of use, not just the structures and vocabulary items themselves.

Source of help for picture preparation

Many of the games in *Games for Language Learning* make use of pictures. Teachers often feel that their own drawing is inadequate and do not attempt to draw anything but the simplest picture of a person. The book, *1000 Pictures for Teachers to Copy*, written by Andrew Wright and published by Collins (1984), might well prove to be a useful source of people, animals, objects and scenes to copy on to worksheets, transparencies or the board.

Language for the organisation of games

We believe that the general language which can be used to organise and to comment on games is as rich in its potential for learning as the specific language of any particular game. In the following section we have listed some of the general language which, in our experience, is useful in organising and commenting on games.

1 General commands, instructions, etc.

TEACHER'S LANGUAGE

Take your time.
Don't be in such a hurry.
Look.
Listen.
Turn round.
Stand in a line.
In twos.
One at a time.

LEARNERS' LANGUAGE

Hurry up.
Be quiet.
Be careful.

2 Organisation

a) Things required for the lesson

TEACHER'S LANGUAGE

| John, | could you would you will you | give out | the pencils, the scissors, the rulers, | please? |

Fetch | the tape recorder | from the storeroom, will you?
       | the projector |

Bring | me | some chalk, | please.
Give | | some paper,
     | | a pencil,

You'll each need | a pencil, a ruler, scissors . . .
You each need | pencils, rulers, scissors . . .
You'll all need
You'll need
You need

Have you each got | a pencil, a ruler, scissors . . .?
Have you all got | pencils, rulers, scissors . . .?
Have you got

Put up your hand(s) | if you need anything.
                  | if you haven't got anything.

What | do you need?
      | haven't you got?

Look. | There are some | here.
      | There's one | over there.

Here you are. Come and get | it.
                            | them.
                            | some.

Help | yourself.
     | yourselves.

One for you, and one for you . . .
One | each.
Two
Three
Four

One between | two.
             | three.
             | four.

One | for each group.
Two
Three

You'll have to share.
Who can lend John a pencil?

Please,	may	I	give out	the	pencils?
	could		fetch		scissors?
	can				rulers?

I'm sorry, I can't find	the pencils.
	the scissors.
	the rulers.
	them.
	any.

I haven't got	a pencil.
	one.
	any.

Please may I have . . .?
(I'm sorry, but) my pencil's broken.

Look.	There's one	over there.
	There it is	on the table.
	There are some	on the desk.
	There they are	by the window.

Here you are.
One for you, and one for you . . .

b) Arrangement of the classroom

Move	the	desk(s)	over there, please.		
Put	your	chair(s)			
Take		things			

Move	the	desk(s)	back where	it	came from.
Put	your	chair(s)		they	
Take		things			

c) *Grouping of learners*

TEACHER'S LANGUAGE

Work with the person sitting next to you.

Work in | twos.
        | threes.
        | fours.
        | your groups.

Split | into your groups (now), please.
Go
Get

John, (would you) sit | next to | Peter, please(?)
                       | behind
                       | in front of

In groups. In your groups.
On your own. By yourself.
You be the group leader.
Would you be the group leader?

Who's next? Whose turn is it?

LEARNERS' LANGUAGE

I want | to work with . . .
I'd like

Let me | have a | turn.
Let's | go.
               | look.

I | haven't had a | turn | (yet).
We | go
                   | look

Whose | turn | is it?
      | go

You do it | first.
          | next.

Let me | do it | first.
Let's | next.

d) Organisation of the game

First,	. . .
Then,	
Next,	
Finally,	

It's your turn. Is it your turn?
It'll be your turn next.
Who hasn't had a turn yet?
You take it in turns.
When he . . . then you must . . .

If you want any help, put up your hand(s).

| Who wants to | try? | |
| | have a go? | |

You must . . .
You've got to . . .

3 Praise, blame, and evaluation

| (I think) | this one | is | better than | that one. |
| | these | are | | those. |

| I don't think | this one | is | as good as | that one. |
| | these | are | | those. |

Good. Quite good. Very good. O.K. Fine. Great.
Well done. Right. Correct.

Wrong. Not right. Not very good.
Not quite right.

| Is | it | all right? |
| | this | |

(I think)	it's good.	
	this is great.	
	they're rubbish.	

4 Interpersonal exchanges

TEACHER'S LANGUAGE

What's wrong? Can I help you?
All right?

LEARNERS' LANGUAGE

Please,	Mr Smith,	. . .
Excuse me,	Mrs Smith,	
	Miss Smith,	
	Dr Smith,	

Would you like to . . .?
Let's . . .
Yes. No. O.K. All right. Certainly not.
Of course.
Wait a moment. Hurry up.
I've finished.

Picture games

We have placed here those games in which the use of pictures plays a major part. There are various types of game in the section. Broadly, they involve: comparing and contrasting pictures; considering differences or similarities; considering possible relationships between pictures, such as narrative sequence; describing key features so that someone else may identify them or represent them in a similar way. Most of the games involve the learners in the relatively free use of all the language at their command. There are games and variations here for all levels of proficiency.

1 That's an unusual view!

Language	Naming and describing objects (*It's a* . . .) or expressing ignorance (*I don't know* or *I've no idea* or *It could be*). In Variation 1, the phrase *It's part of* . . . is used.
Skills	Listening and speaking.
Control	Guided.
Level	Beginners.
Time	10–15 minutes.
Materials	Chalkboard or OHP. In the variations, magazine pictures.

Preparation

Prepare a few drawings of unusual views of common objects on sheets of paper or for the OHP. (See illustration.)

Procedure

Class work, optionally leading to group work.

Draw several examples of unusual views of objects on the board or

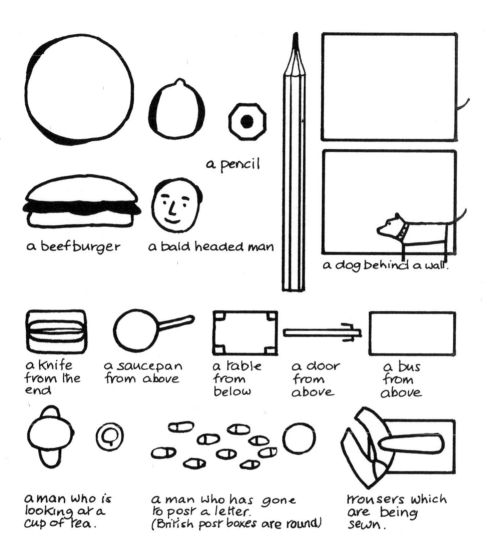

a pencil

a beefburger   a bald headed man

a dog behind a wall.

a knife from the end   a saucepan from above   a table from below   a door from above   a bus from above

a man who is looking at a cup of tea.   a man who has gone to post a letter. (British post boxes are round)   trousers which are being sewn.

the OHP. Ask what they are and, once identified, draw or show a picture of the same object from a more familiar angle, e.g.

Teacher: What's this?
Learner 1: It's a woman's face.
Teacher: She hasn't got any eyes or a nose!
Learner 2: It's a beefburger.
Teacher: Yes. It's a beefburger from above.

Ask the learners to prepare ideas of their own for a few minutes and then to challenge the rest of the class or group. If the learners cannot answer, they must say 'I don't know' or 'I've no idea'.

Variation 1
Class work, optionally leading to group work.
   Use pictures from magazines, etc. These may be unusual views of objects or parts of objects which you have cut out.
   If you show parts of objects the learners should say 'part of', e.g.
Learner 1: It's part of a wheel.

Variation 2
Class work, optionally leading to group work.
   Show a small part of a picture as you pull it from an envelope. Let the class guess what it might be. Alternatively, you may show a small part of a picture on the OHP by covering it with a piece of paper that has a hole cut in it. The hole may be a slit, a circle, a square – or shaped like a keyhole.

2   Predicting pictures

Language	Future with *going to*. Exclamations of pleasure (e.g. *Marvellous!*) and of regret (e.g. *What a pity!*).
Skills	Listening and speaking.
Control	Guided.
Level	Beginners/intermediate.
Time	10–15 minutes.
Materials	Magazine or catalogue pictures, pieces of card.

Preparation

Collect 15–20 pictures of objects from a catalogue or magazine. Alternatively you may draw them. (The pictures from 'Happy twins' (Game 3) may be used.) Mount your pictures on pieces of card which are all the same size.

Procedure

Class, group or pair work.
   The learners should first familiarise themselves with the pictures on the cards. Then mix all the pictures and lay them in a pile, face down.

Players take it in turns to try to predict the next picture: if they are right they take it and if they are wrong they place it at the bottom of the pack, e.g.

Learner 1: It's going to be a typewriter. No! What a pity! (What a shame!) (*puts it underneath the pack*)

Learner 2: It's going to be a kettle. Yes, it's mine! Marvellous!

3 Happy twins

Language	Describing pictures of objects and people.
Skills	Listening and speaking. Variation 3 also includes reading.
Control	Free.
Level	Intermediate.
Time	10–15 minutes.
Materials	Pictures, either from magazines or drawn; envelopes; written instructions.

Preparation

Collect 16–20 pictures of single objects or people from magazines, or draw them. Most of the pictures should form pairs of *identical* objects or people. Mount them on pieces of card which are all the same size. Put all the pictures into an envelope, together with the instructions for the game. Note how many pairs there are. One set of pictures will be needed for each pair of learners.

Procedure

Pair work.

The aim is for two players, working together, to collect all the pairs.

The pictures should be mixed and placed in a pile face down. Each player takes it in turn to pick up a card *without showing it to the other*. Then each player describes his/her own card *without letting the other see*. The players can also ask each other questions.

If they decide they have a pair, they place them on the table. If the cards *are* a pair they put them on one side. If the cards are not a pair they put them back into the pack.

Variation 1
Class work.

You must make enough pairs of pictures for each learner to have *one* picture. For example, if you have 20 students you must have ten pairs of pictures. (The pictures can be *very* simple and very small! You can easily get ten small drawings on one sheet of A4 paper which you then photocopy to get a pair. If the drawings are all similar it will be more difficult and produce more discussion! Cut the sheets of paper up and you will have 20 drawings.)

Give each learner one picture. Each learner must then find which other learner has the same picture. The level of difficulty of language is determined by the drawings you choose to do.

Variation 2
Pair work.

Ten or twelve pictures must be laid at random face down in front of each pair of learners. Among the ten or twelve pictures are a few identical pairs and others which are similar. Each player must pick up one picture. Through discussion they must find out whether they have an identical pair. When they decide that they have or have not got an identical pair, they may look at the pictures.

If they have correctly judged the pictures to be a pair, they should put them on one side. If they are not an identical pair, the pictures should be laid down again, face down, and all the pictures shuffled around at random. When they have correctly identified all the pairs, the game is over.

Of course, you can make the game shorter by having fewer pictures! You can make it more difficult by having many similar pictures!

Variation 3
Pair or group work.

Instead of pictures you can give each learner a piece of paper on which are written a number of individual words or sentences. All the papers should have some words in common; there will be only two of each kind.

4 Describe and draw a picture

Language	Describing pictures, asking questions, making comparisons, encouraging, praising, criticising.
Skills	Listening and speaking, and, in Variation 3, reading and writing.
Control	Free.
Level	Intermediate/advanced.
Time	15–20 minutes.
Materials	Magazine pictures or line drawings, paper and pencils. Chalkboard in Variation 5.

Preparation

Select from magazines any pictures which show a number of different objects. The objects should be clear in shape and the pictures should preferably not include people. It is amusing if the objects are bizarre in some way – but this is not essential.

Alternatively, the language can be limited if the original is a simple line drawing *or* the language may be specialised if the original is a technical diagram.

See examples on p. 21.

For each pair of learners you will need one picture, a piece of paper and a pencil.

Procedure

Pair work.

One learner describes the picture to the other who must try to draw it. *The other must not see the original,* e.g.

Learner 1: There is a square table in the picture. It is in the middle of the picture.
Learner 2: About here?
Learner 1: Yes . . . well, a little further down.
Learner 2: Is it like that?
Learner 1: No, not quite, the legs are too long.

When the 'artist' and his 'patron' have done as much as they can, the original and the copy should be compared, e.g.

Learner 2: Oh, the table legs are too long!
Learner 1: I told you they were. But you wouldn't change them!

Variation 1
Pair work
   The 'artist' is asked by the 'patron' to add details to an existing picture (which you have supplied). The detail might be, for example, buttons on a coat, hair, windows. The detail might be colour.
   To produce this nearly complete picture you would have to take a line drawing and make enough photocopies of it for half the class. Then white out parts of the same drawing (with typist's correction fluid) before making copies for the other half of the class. The 'patron' would get the complete picture and the 'artist' the incomplete picture.

Variation 2
Class work.
   Instead of the instructions and description of the picture being given by a learner, they can be given by you (or a tape recording) for the whole class. Each learner draws his/her own picture.

Variation 3
Pair work.
   This variation involves descriptive writing. Each learner is given a picture to describe in writing. When the descriptions are ready, they are exchanged with a neighbour, who must then try to make a drawing based on the description. When the drawings are complete, they may be compared with the originals and the differences discussed.

Variation 4
Pair work.
   The 'patron' describes an object but does *not* describe its function or name it. The 'artist' tries to draw the object as it is described and may ask questions to improve the representation.

Group work.
   Alternatively, the game may be played in a group with two or three players listening to the description, watching the drawing and guessing what the object might be.

Variation 5
Class work leading to pair work.
   Draw, or ask a learner to draw, a picture on the board.
   Now ask another learner to draw on the board a copy of the first drawing. As he/she does so, encourage the class to make helpful comments, e.g.

Class: His head is too big.
His legs aren't long enough.
His body is too fat.
The stripes are too narrow.
His trousers are too wide.
His face is too ugly.
That's better.
Good.

Organise pair work in the usual way. Each learner should draw a picture and take it in turns to copy his/her partner's.

5 What's the difference?

Language	Describing pictures of objects and people, asking questions, making comparisons, e.g. *bigger than, too big, not big enough.*
Skills	Listening and speaking.
Control	Free.
Level	Intermediate/advanced.
Time	5–15 minutes.
Materials	Magazine pictures or line drawings. For Variation 1, flashcards, OHP, or photocopies.

Preparation

Each pair of learners will need two pictures or sets of pictures which are very similar. The differences between them must be describable by the learners!

Possible sources and types of picture:
a) Magazine pictures; for example, two pictures of different though similar bathrooms, or houses, or groups of people.
b) A line drawing, perhaps from a magazine. Photocopy the drawing then white out some parts. You can draw in alternative bits if you wish. Then photocopy the photocopy. In this way you will have two very similar drawings.

c) Instead of *one* pair of drawings you can have a lot of them. And instead of being, for example, naturalistic representations they can be *very* simple or even abstract designs. *Ten* such pictures fit on to one sheet of A4. (See illustration.)

Examples of naturalistic and abstract drawings

SHEET A
SHEET B

Each learner in a pair gets one of these sheets. Thus, for a class of 20 learners you would need ten of Sheet A and ten of Sheet B.

d) Of course *any* information which is similar, though not identical, may be used. The information may be verbal or numerical instead of pictorial. It *could* be all three!

Procedure

Pair work.

Divide the class into pairs. (If you have not got enough pictures for everyone, then some pairs can play another pair work game.) Each player gets one picture and does *not* see his/her partner's picture. Both players may describe their own picture and/or ask questions of the other. The aim is for the players to find the differences between the two pictures.

Finally the two pictures are compared and discussed further.

Variation 1
Class work or pair work.

Copy, or trace, a drawing (a comic cartoon is often suitable). Then make another copy, but deliberately introduce seven or eight differences. You can do this by omitting parts of the original, by making additions, or by making small changes. The two drawings can be presented on flashcards, OHP transparencies, or on photocopied sheets.

The drawings on p. 26 show how this can be done simply.

The learners study the pictures. As soon as someone sees a difference, he describes it to the class, e.g.

In the second picture, the big monkey's thumb is longer.
the mountain is higher.
the wheel on the lorry is smaller.
the little monkey's ears are bigger.
the man hasn't got a hat on.
there is no headlight on the lorry.
the big monkey is holding a banana.

More advanced learners could be asked to write down all the differences they can find before the oral discussion.

Learners can play this game in pairs, making their own drawings.

Variation 2
Pair work.

If you have given copies of the same pair of pictures to everyone in the class, you can try the following organisation.

After five minutes ask one learner from each pair to move to the next pair. The new pair should compare their conclusions concerning the similarities and the differences between their two pictures. Then, they should continue to try to find more. After a further five minutes ask the learner who moved before to move again. Once more, established information is exchanged and then the discussion continues.

6 Drawing blind

Language	Giving instructions, referring to objects, positions, etc., criticising, encouraging, e.g. *Draw a tree on the right . . . Make it bigger . . . That's right . . .*
Skills	Listening and speaking.
Control	Free.
Level	Intermediate/advanced.
Time	5–10 minutes.
Materials	Chalkboard, OHP or large piece of paper.

Preparation

Prepare a large drawing on paper or OHP transparency. The drawing should be of one or two quite simple and clearly defined objects. See example on p. 28.

Procedure

Class work.

A volunteer is blindfolded and, without ever seeing your picture, tries to draw it on the board following instructions called from the class.

7 Arrange the pictures

Language	Describing pictures of objects and people (e.g. *He's holding a pipe*), giving instructions concerning position and sequence, asking questions, encouraging, etc.
Skills	Listening and speaking. Variations 5, 6 and 7 also include writing.
Control	Free.
Level	Intermediate/advanced.
Time	5–15 minutes.
Materials	Pictures or line drawings. In Variation 4, a collection of objects.

Preparation

You need two sets of the same pictures. One set should be in a fixed order but the other should not be. If you can find two copies of the same magazine, holiday brochure or comic, one page of pictures can be kept complete and the other cut up. Alternatively, the pictures may be drawn.

Procedure

Pair work.

Give the complete set of pictures to one player and the separate pictures to the other. *The second player must not see the complete version.* The first player then describes the pictures, beginning with the first one, and tells the second player the order to arrange them in. The second player may ask questions, e.g.

Learner 1: There's a man in the first picture. He's holding a pipe but he's not smoking it.
Learner 2: (*Picks up the wrong one.*)
Learner 1: No, I said he *isn't* smoking his pipe.
Learner 2: Oh, sorry. Is it this one with the green curtains?
Learner 1: Yes. Good. Now the second one . . .

The game may, of course, be followed by a short discussion of what happened in the pictures.

Variation 1
Pair work.

The game may be *organised* differently. The two learners can be seated back to back so neither can see what the other is doing.

Variation 2
Group work leading to class work.

DESCRIBE AND SEQUENCE: Cut the picture-strip sequence into the individual pictures. Give one picture to each group. (If there are extra pictures keep them on one side.)

Each group studies their picture and tries to guess what story it is a part of. The group should write down their idea. Then the pictures are exchanged and each group tries to imagine what the story might be, based on the picture they have and the one they had previously. When all the pictures have been exchanged and examined, the groups rearrange themselves so that there is one person from each of the previous groups in the new groups.

Each learner then reports what story is proposed by his/her former group. Each proposal is considered and evaluated by the group as a whole.

Finally, the teacher presents the pictures in order and tells the story.

If there are any pictures from the strip which have not been examined, all the class can be invited to guess the ending based on them.

Variation 3
Group work as part of class work.

DESCRIBE AND SEQUENCE: Each group is given *one* picture from a sequence. Once the groups have studied their picture and attempted to interpret what is happening in it, one learner is sent to another group to learn from them what their picture shows. This information is reported back to the group and in a similar way information is taken from each of the other groups. Through discussion each group attempts to evolve the correct sequence of pictures. The various interpretations of the groups are then compared.

Variation 4
Pair or group work.

DESCRIBE AND BUILD: You will need some objects rather than pictures for this game. The objects might be:
– a set of toy bricks

– parts of a construction set
– various toy cars, houses, people, trees, etc.
– a set of Cuisenaire rods.
You must also make a diagram showing the completed arrangement of the various elements.

One learner (or a pair) has the completed diagram or drawing. He/she does not show it to the others. He/she must direct the others, verbally, how to arrange the various objects. The others may ask questions.

Variation 5
Group work.

DESCRIBE THE JIGSAW: For one group you must cut up a magazine picture and give each learner one or two pieces. Each learner then writes a description of his/her piece of the picture without letting the others see it.

Collect in the pieces of picture.

The group should then consider the descriptions of each piece of picture and try to compile a single description of the whole picture.

Note: You could complicate the work by *not* giving out all the pieces!

Variation 6
Class work and pair work.

DESCRIBE THE JIGSAW: For this variation you must cut one large magazine picture or poster into six or seven pieces. Show four of the pieces to the class. Each pair should make notes and try to imagine what the whole picture looks like. Each pair should write down their description and then, through class discussion, find out what the others have thought.

Variation 7
Class work and pair or individual work.

DESCRIBE THE JIGSAW: Cut up one large magazine picture or poster into a lot of small pieces – enough small pieces for each learner in the class to have one.

All the learners must then circulate in the class examining each of the other pieces of the picture and making notes on them. Finally, each learner must try to imagine and then make a written description of the complete picture. Considering all the notes made, imagining the complete picture and writing a description can be done as pair work.

8 Describe and identify the picture

Language	Describing details of a picture; Variations 1 and 2 entail imagining a dialogue and a person's thoughts respectively; Variation 3 entails asking questions.
Skills	Listening and speaking. Variations 1 and 2 also include writing.
Control	Free.
Level	Intermediate/advanced.
Time	15–20 minutes.
Materials	Pictures or drawings.

Preparation

Either you need one picture with a lot of detail in it: for example, the famous Bruegel painting which shows children playing 60 different games would be ideal! Or you need a collection of pictures which might be, for example, a page of comic strip pictures. You, or one of your students, could draw about 20 small drawings on one piece of paper.

Procedure

Pair work.

One learner thinks of one detail and then describes it so that his/her partner can identify it by pointing to or marking the picture.

Variation 1
Group work.

The group should have either a large picture with a lot of people in it or a number of different pictures of people who might be talking together. Each pair (or threesome) in the group, without telling the others, chooses two people in the picture who might be having a conversation.

The pair devise and write out a conversation and perform it for the others. The others must say which two people in the picture were being represented.

Variation 2
Group work.

As above, but instead of working in pairs, each learner imagines what one person in the picture might be thinking. Once more, the others must guess which person in the picture was being represented.

Variation 3
Pair work.

One learner thinks of *one* detail in the big picture (or one detail in one of the strip pictures or one of your own drawn pictures). The other learner asks questions to find out which detail his/her partner is thinking about.

9 Are you a good detective?

Language	Comparing a written description of a picture with the picture itself, identifying and discussing discrepancies, and composing an accurate description.
Skills	All.
Control	Guided.
Level	Intermediate/advanced.
Time	20–40 minutes.
Materials	A photograph or series of photographs; a written account; paper and pencils.

Preparation

Take an interesting photograph from a newspaper or magazine, then write an account of the event shown in the photograph which, in several respects, is at variance with the evidence of the photograph.

Procedure

Class work.

The learners can discuss with you the contradictions between the photograph and the written account before going on to write an account which does not contradict the photograph.

Variation
Class work.

If you are trying to introduce a class to writing narratives based on a series of pictures, you will find this game useful. Write a description of the pictures, using the sort of language you would like the learners to use, but making a number of factual errors.

The learners compare the pictures and your text, reading the text aloud until they see a mistake. They then correct the sentence containing the mistake orally. When all the mistakes have been corrected in this way, the learners can write a corrected narrative.

10   Picture/text matching

Language	Matching words (single words, sentences and paragraphs) to pictures; discussing; and, in the variation, writing biographical notes (age, likes and dislikes, beliefs, occupation, etc.).
Skills	Reading, with listening and speaking. The variation also entails writing.
Control	Controlled.
Level	All.
Time	Depends on the length and complexity of the texts.
Materials	Pictures and pieces of card.

Preparation

You must collect four or five pictures and write a description of each picture on a separate piece of paper or card. If you wish to increase the complexity then include similar, though not identical, information in each text.

Of course, the preparation could be carried out by the students themselves and be used to challenge each other. Four or five pictures and texts are enough for one pair.

Procedure

Individual or pair work.

This is one of the great families of games in language learning! There are suitable variations of this game for students at all levels of proficiency. In the most elementary of all the variations of this game the learner is given four or five separate picture cards and on separate cards the words which name the objects in the pictures. The aim of the learner is to match the appropriate text to each picture. (See illustration.)

Printer Lid →

He is a small man
and he is wearing a
tall, black hat and
a wide, big coat. He is
being followed!

If the printer lid is an obstacle when removing the shipping screws, be sure to take off the printer lid by observing the following steps. Rough or careless handling of the printer lid may result in damage to, or even breakage of, its hinges.

a cup

The same procedure can be used at any level of proficiency. At a slightly higher level the student can be asked to match sentences to pictures and the teacher may ensure that there are some things common to several of the pictures in order to make the matching more difficult. The texts could be dialogue, instead of description.

At a higher level of proficiency in, for example, the teaching of English to engineers, five diagrams of electric pumps and five detailed texts might have to be matched. In this case the students themselves should be asked to prepare both illustrations and texts!

Variation
Pair or group work leading to class work.

Give each pair (or group) a magazine picture which is, effectively, a study of someone. The person should not be known to the learners. The pair (or group) must study the portrait and try to imagine as much about the person as possible: age, work, likes and dislikes, character, rich or poor or average, beliefs about society and social behaviour, etc. These interpretations should be written down by each learner: the learners in the pair (or group) may work together on the text.

You then collect all the portraits and display them (by use of drawing pins or adhesive). When you have done this, all the learners circulate inspecting the pictures for a few minutes.

Then take the first description at random, read it out (you would probably say who wrote the description). The aim is for the other pairs (or groups) to decide which of the portraits is being referred to. You may complicate the activity by adding more portraits than used by the pairs (or groups)).

Note: We feel that there is a temptation in this activity for the learners to resort to stereotyping. In real life a poet may look like the stereotype of a brutish criminal and a person with a romantic and wistful face may have committed many cruel actions. You might feel inclined to discuss this with the learners.

Psychology games

In this section we have included a variety of games which might all lead to a greater awareness of the workings of the human mind and senses. This is an area of interest for everyone, in which there is much individual variation of opinion and experience. Our games exploit this fact in ways which encourage concentration and language use.

11   Telepathy

Language	Asking questions about the content of pictures, e.g. *Is he running?*
Skills	Listening and speaking, with reading in the variation.
Control	Controlled.
Level	Beginners.
Time	10–15 minutes for class work. 10–15 minutes for pair work.
Materials	Picture cards.

Preparation

You will need six to eight picture cards of, for example, actions. It is better to have all the actions in the picture done by *one* sex, so this element need not be established.

Procedure

Class work leading to pair work.

Make sure the learners know the picture cards in your hand. They should be able to remember all of them. Then ask if anyone believes in telepathy. Discuss telepathy with the class in the mother tongue for a few moments, raising interest in whether or not there is any truth in it. Say that you will do an experiment. Select one of the picture cards at random and show it to only half the class. Tell them they must concentrate on the card, and send out 'telepathic signals'.

Tell the other half of the class that you will give them three chances to receive the 'telepathic signals'. In our experience it is astonishing how often the message seems to be received! It is then inevitable for people to feel the need to try it again. Do it perhaps five times. Each time record if the 'message' was received within three attempts, e.g.

Learner 1: Is he swimming?
Teacher: No.
Learner 2: Is he running?
Teacher: Yes! Well done.

Then suggest that the same experiment is done in pairs. Each learner should draw three or four stickmen showing different actions. (Or they might write down three or four short sentences.) Then one learner in each pair takes both sets of drawings, and, hiding them from the other learner behind a book, places his/her finger on one of them. The other learner then has three guesses. You could ask them to do the experiment ten times with utmost concentration. And they should record each time the right guess is made within the first three attempts.

Variation
Class work.

Ask if anyone in the class believes in telepathy. (You will probably do this in the mother tongue.) Say that you intend to carry out an experiment to test telepathic communication.

Write four short texts on the board.

Ask one learner, who is prepared to be a 'medium', to think of one of the texts.

Ask the rest of the class, whether they believe in telepathy or not, to try to concentrate on which they think the 'medium' has chosen and to write down that particular text.

After two minutes, ask each learner to read out his/her text, in turn. (In this activity it is remarkable how everyone *wants* to listen to everyone else. Everyone wants to be right!)

Ask someone to stand by the chalkboard and to place a tick beside each text as it is referred to.

When all the ticks have been added up, ask the 'medium' to say which text he/she was thinking of. Decide whether he/she has managed to transmit his/her thoughts!

12   Visual perception of length

Language	Making statements about length, using comparatives (*longer*, *shorter*) and superlatives (*longest*, *shortest*); using possessives (e.g. *John's line*) and names of colours; expressing conjecture (*I think . . .*).
Skills	Listening and speaking.
Control	Guided.
Level	Beginners.
Time	2–3 minutes for class work. 20 minutes for pair work.
Materials	For class work you need a chalkboard and a large sheet of paper, or the OHP, coloured chalks or pens (4 or 5), and a ruler. For pair work you need paper, coloured pens and rulers.

Preparation

Collect all the necessary materials.

Procedure

Class work leading to pair work.

Four or five learners take it in turns to draw a line on the board. Each line should be in a different colour, of a different length and be straight. (The lengths should not be too varied.) It helps the game if the lines are crossed.

Challenge the class to judge which is the longest, and which the shortest line, e.g.

Teacher: Which is the longest line, Rachel?
Learner 1: John's line.
Teacher: What do you think, Robin?
Learner 2: I think Mary's line is the longest.

You will find it natural to use the comparative forms as you discuss the opinions put forward.

Teacher: Don't you think the red line is longer than the green line, Robin?

To encourage the learners to use the comparative form:

Teacher: I think the blue line is longer than the brown line. What do you think, David?

Learner: I think it's shorter.

After some further discussion you might then ask each learner to write down his/her judgements, e.g.

The green line is the shortest line.
The red line is longer than the green line.
The brown line is longer than the red line.
The white line is the longest.

Finally, measure the lines and write the measurements next to them.

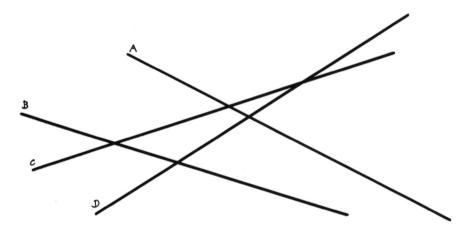

Pair work.

    Each learner draws, with a ruler, a number of coloured lines on a piece of paper. Below the lines he/she writes a number of sentences, some true and some deliberately false, concerning the relative lengths, e.g.

The red line (A) is longer than the green line (C).
The brown line (B) is longer than the black line (D).
The green line is shorter than the brown line.

The pieces of paper are then interchanged and the receiver must decide, judging by eye, which of the statements are true and which false.

Variation 1
Pair work.
   Instead of drawing the lines at random across each other, draw them parallel in pairs and add arrow heads.

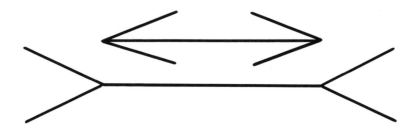

The open arrowhead makes the lower line appear to be longer than the upper one.

   Each learner should draw three or four pairs of lines with a ruler and make them either the same length or very slightly different. Next to (or below) each pair he/she should write a statement which is true or false, for example: 'Line A is longer than line B.' Once more the drawings and sentences are exchanged and the receiver must decide, judging by eye, which of the statements are true and which are false.

Variation 2
Pair work.
   An alternative diagram can give the impression that the left-hand vertical line is shorter than the right-hand vertical when it may be the same in length or even a little shorter or longer. Once more, each learner should draw several of these diagrams, adjusting them slightly and then making a true or false statement in writing which the partner must judge.

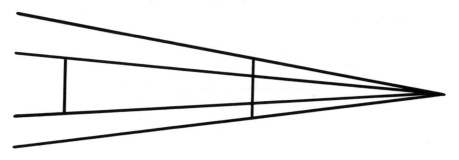

Variation 3
Pair work.

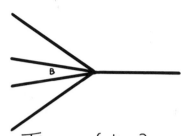

Angle A is greater than angle B.   True or false?

Once more, each learner should draw several of these diagrams, adjusting them slightly and then making a true or a false statement which the partner must judge.

Variation 4
Pair work.

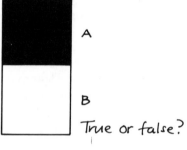

Area A is bigger than area B.   True or false?

Once more, each learner should draw several of these diagrams, adjusting them slightly and then making a true or a false statement which the partner must judge.

Variation 5
Pair work.

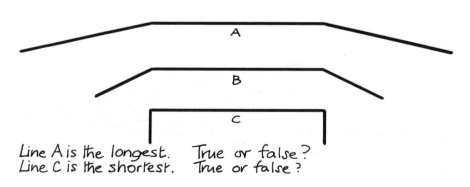

Line A is the longest.   True or false?
Line C is the shortest.   True or false?

Once more, each learner should draw several of these diagrams, adjusting them slightly and then making a true or a false statement which the partner must judge.

13   The old woman and the young woman

Language	Identifying physical features in pictures (e.g. *This is the/her nose*, etc.). There is an opportunity for using expressions of astonishment (e.g. *Oh yes!* or *Good Lord!*).
Skills	Listening and speaking.
Control	Guided.
Level	Beginners.
Time	5–10 minutes.
Materials	You will need a slide or a large copy of the picture on p. 44.

Preparation

Prepare the copy of the picture.

Procedure

Class work.

Show the picture without comment for about one minute. Some of the class will see an *old* woman and some will see a *young* woman.

Ask the class what they can see in the picture and show some astonishment that there are quite contradictory opinions about it. You might ask how many can see the young woman and how many can see the old woman.

Finally, ask someone to indicate on the picture the person that *they* can see, e.g.

Learner: This is the nose.

This is the chin.

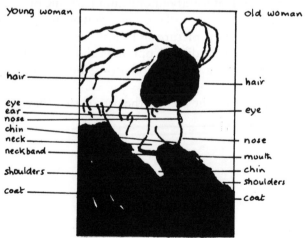

14   Blobs

Language	Describing, particularly by analogy, e.g. *It looks like a bird . . .*
Skills	Listening and speaking.
Control	Guided, except in the variation, where less control of language is possible or desirable.
Level	Beginners/intermediate, except for the variation, which is aimed at advanced learners.
Time	10–15 minutes of playing time. Allow another 10–15 minutes if the learners are going to make their own blob pictures.
Materials	Various (see *Preparation*).

Preparation

The aim in the preparation is to make an abstract collection of shapes and marks. You may do this in any of the following ways:
a) Arrange a number of pieces of torn paper, sand, string, paint, etc. on the screen of the OHP.
b) Splatter, pat and dab some coloured paints or inks on to a large piece of paper.
c) Scribble and smudge pencils and crayons on paper.
d) Place a piece of thin paper on an irregular rough surface and rub a soft black crayon on it.

Procedure

Class work leading to pair work.
   Show the blob picture to the class. Ask if they can see anything in it. If no ideas are forthcoming you might ask, e.g.
Teacher: Can you see an animal?
    or: I think this looks like a bird. It's flying. Here are its wings. Here's its head and its beak, etc.

When a learner sees something in the blob pictures, ask him/her to identify the various parts.

Pair work.
   Learners can make their own blob pictures using the methods

45

described above. They can then discuss what they see, and write on the picture labelling the different parts of the thing they can see.

Variation
Class work.

The famous Swiss psychiatrist Rorschach believed that people's interpretations of blob pictures reveal their personalities. He believed that a concern with white spaces shows a negative attitude; concern with bright colour shows an emotional character; concern with various tones shows a trivial and vacillating character; concern with minute detail shows a compulsive nature. These beliefs might be used with advanced learners to stimulate a discussion of people's interpretations and their personality.

15 How quickly can you see?

Language	Describing pictures, with special use of the past continuous (e.g. *He was running*).
Skills	Listening and speaking.
Control	Guided.
Level	All.
Time	5–10 minutes.
Materials	You need a collection of pictures no bigger than magazine page size. The pictures may be photographs or drawings and may be on paper, OHP transparency or slide.

Preparation

Collect the pictures.

If you are concentrating on a particular language-teaching point, then you must collect the pictures accordingly (see examples in *Procedure*).

Procedure

Class work leading to pair work.

Explain that you are going to test the learners' ability to see at great speed. It is a challenge of their power to react quickly. Flash a picture at the class, first making sure that everyone has a chance to see it – there should be no heads in the way and the angle should not be too acute for players on each side of the class.

(Picture of a man running)
Teacher: What was he doing?
Learner: (He was) running.

(Picture of five sheep)
Teacher: What did you see?
Learner: Some sheep.
Teacher: How many did you see?
Learner: Five.

(Picture of two men)
Teacher: What did you see?
Learner: Two men.
Teacher: What were they doing?
Learner: One was standing and the other was sitting.
Teacher: Which man was standing?
Learner: The one who was wearing a hat.

(Picture of two girls)
Teacher: What did you see?
Learner: Two girls.
Teacher: Which one was the taller?
Learner: The one in the blue hat.

(Picture of a packet of cigarettes)
Teacher: What did you see?
Learner: A packet of cigarettes.
Teacher: Was it a new one or had it been opened?
Learner: It had been opened.

The game can later be played in pairs, using small pictures.

16 Faces and character

Language	Describing people, speculating about age, character, etc. (e.g. *He might be . . .*).
Skills	Listening and speaking.
Control	Free.
Level	Intermediate/advanced.
Time	5 minutes for a discussion of each photograph you choose to show.
Materials	Photographs or slides.

Preparation

For class work you will need a minimum of three or four photographs of people you know or know about. The pictures should be large enough for class use. (Projected slides would be ideal.)

For pair work, the pupils must be equipped in a similar way. They could be asked to bring pictures from home of their family, friends or anyone else who will be unknown to other learners in the class.

Procedure

Class work leading to pair work.

First discuss with the class how reliable people's appearance is as a guide to their age, interests, background, character, etc. You might tell them that it was commonly believed in the last century that one could recognise a criminal by the shape of his ears! Then say that you will show a picture of someone you know well and that you will ask the class to suggest as much as they can to you about the person. Finally confirm, qualify or reject these speculations by describing the person yourself.

17   Visual imagery

Language	Using any appropriate language to describe mental pictures.
Skills	Speaking and/or writing.
Control	Free.
Level	Advanced.
Time	5–10 minutes.
Materials	None, except for Variation 3, which requires a picture or book.

Preparation

None.

Procedure

Class work.

Psychologists of perception have established that the majority of people see pictures in the mind quite apart from their dreams. Most people see these pictures just before going to sleep. However, it is quite possible to see them at other times, when the eyes are closed.

This activity needs considerable understanding between members of the class as it involves personal and, perhaps, private feelings. If you have a suitable class then you might try it.

Here is an example of what might be 'seen':

I can see waves crashing on the shore and palm trees bending in the wind. Now I am looking down into some water plants. I can see a nest with pale blue eggs in it.

Encourage the learners to describe, in spoken or written form, what they 'see' when they close their eyes.

Variation 1
Class work or pair work.

It is very hard for people to concentrate on their inner visual images whilst remaining awake and aware. You can help your learners to do this and provide a rewarding personal, as well as shared, experience.

It is, of course, essential to have a peaceful, relaxed atmosphere in the classroom. You must create the necessary mood by your tone of voice and through your quiet explanation of what is going to happen. Hypnotists will sometimes go so far as to name each part of the subject's body which should relax and grow heavier. Your aim is similar, to focus the learners' concentration on the inner rather than the outer world. The easiest thing to do is to describe something so that each person can picture it in their mind. Speak in a relaxed way, pausing between each sentence. Do not be too specific in the detail you give, for example, the colour of the horse or whether there are clouds and birds in the sky. Here is one for you to try:

Teacher: Now I'm going to describe something to you. It's a horse. You can see all of the horse. It is standing on the top of a grassy rise. There is a breeze. The longer grasses are bending in the breeze and the mane of the horse is also lifting a little and its long, fair tail is whisking lightly around its legs.

Having achieved the necessary state of mind and having 'seen' the horse the learners may well be reluctant to 'come back' to the classroom! You might describe another image.

Then, ask the learners to tell their neighbours what they saw. At first they may appear to have had an identical image. Through discussion, the horse and the way it was standing, the field and the other surrounding features may prove to have been seen differently.

Note: This basic version of the activity can be done in pairs.

Variation 2
Class work.

Comparatively few people can *hear* sound in their mind and very few can touch, taste or smell. With the cooperation of the class, you could conduct an experiment finding out how many learners can imagine the examples you give them.

For example, imagine a sound, a smell or the feel of an object:

Teacher: Can you hear a baby cry, a trumpet, the wind blowing strongly?
Can you smell a flower, a perfume, new bread?
Can you feel a cold marble surface, a mohair jersey, someone's cheek?

It is interesting to note the number of people who can imagine these sensations so vividly that they seem real.

Variation 3
Class work.

Eidetic imagery is remembered visual imagery. Some people have the ability to remember complete pages of a book and can read a text from the image of it in their head.

Discuss this with the class. Then conduct an experiment. You might show them a picture or ask them to look at the back of the room or at a certain page in a textbook. Give them a few seconds only. Tell them to try not to use the verbal memory but just to 'photograph' the image into their minds. Then ask them to write down all they can see in their minds afterwards.

18 Palmistry

Language	Describing people's characters, using the language of amazement, concern, condolence, etc. The future is referred to, using both *will* and *going to*.
Skills	Listening and speaking.
Control	Free.
Level	Advanced.
Time	30–60 minutes.
Materials	A big copy of the hand on p. 53, on a large piece of paper or on an OHP transparency.

Preparation

Prepare the picture.

Procedure

Class work combined with pair or individual work.

Ask the learners to trace round their own hands, to draw in the lines and, referring to your big picture of a hand, to interpret the lines and write a description of their own characters. With the class as a whole, debate the extent to which these descriptions and predictions might be accurate.

Additionally, you might be able to photocopy various people's hands, and ask the class to interpret them and try to name the owners!

If you and your learners are interested in what palmists say about hands, then we recommend you buy a book on the subject, for example

What Your Hands Reveal by Jo Sheridan, published by Mayflower. We have found that even people who do not believe there is any truth in the analysis of the palmist will be intrigued and pay attention. Here are a few notes to whet your appetite!

Heart line
If the Heart line begins between the index finger and the middle finger it means that reason controls feeling. A strong line means you are warm, a weak line means you are reluctant to give your love or that you are rather cool. Each small line attached to the Heart line means a moment of attraction towards someone or even a flirtation or an affair.

Head line
If the Head line starts with the Life line it means good control. If the Head line drops sharply down then it indicates little power of resistance and a tendency to depression. A long, strong Head line means you are very intelligent.

Life line
The longer your Life line, the longer you will live.

Saturn line
If the Saturn line is clear and goes as far as the middle finger, you will be successful.

Sun line
A weak Sun line means you have no clear idea of what it is you want to do with your life. A double Sun line means creativity, success and prosperity. If the line starts from the Head line success will come in middle life.

Mercury line
A long Mercury line means you have a good memory and that you understand people very well. If it starts at the Life line you have artistic understanding and wealth. A short line means you have problems at work.

Neptune line
A Neptune line means imagination. If it begins inside the Life line it means you have a tendency to take alcohol or drugs. And a broken Neptune line means a lot of imagination and criminal tendencies!

The size and shape of the hand and each of the fingers are also thought to provide information about our natures!

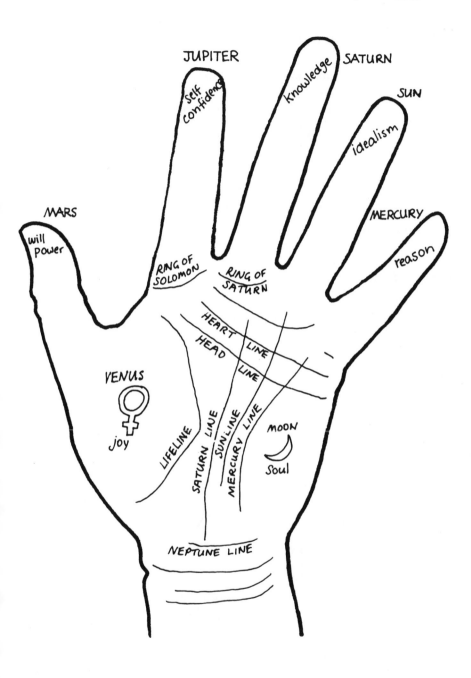

JUPITER
SATURN
SUN
MERCURY
MARS

Self confidence
Knowledge
idealism
reason
will power

RING OF SOLOMON
RING OF SATURN

HEART LINE
HEAD LINE

VENUS
joy

LIFELINE
SATURN LINE
SUN LINE
MERCURY LINE

MOON
Soul

NEPTUNE LINE

19   A memory system

Language	Vocabulary revision. At a more advanced level this game can lead to the need to describe in detail bizarre pictures and to a discussion of the nature of memory!
Skills	Listening and speaking, with some writing.
Control	Guided.
Level	Intermediate/advanced.
Time	20–30 minutes to play it and discuss it.
Materials	Paper and pencils.

Preparation

You must learn the trick before the lesson. Our experience shows that *most* people can master the trick in spite of their having a low opinion of their powers of memory!

The aim is to remember any 16 nouns which are given to you. The method is as follows: you memorise 16 objects, one for each number, *before* the lesson. This is easy because you choose objects which look like the numbers. (See illustration.)

1 match	**2** swan	**3** clubs	**4** chair
5 star	**6** elephant	**7** flag	**8** hourglass

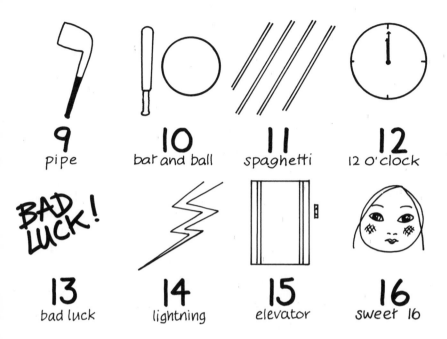

9 pipe

10 bat and ball

11 spaghetti

12 12 o'clock

13 bad luck

14 lightning

15 elevator

16 sweet 16

In order to use this system as a memory aid you must relate visually each word you are given to one of the objects fixed in your mind. The more bizarre your association, the more easily you will remember the words given to you. For example, if the class have chosen 'shoe' for number one, then you might visualise a shoe full of matches. If a number two is a table, you might imagine swan-shaped table legs.

The idea for this memory trick is based on ancient methods for memorising stories and accounts. These methods were common before the introduction of printing and the availability of the book as a memory store.

Warning: We feel this technique has more curiosity value than usefulness! You fix the words to an inflexible filing system. The technique lends itself to the memorising of lists of individual items but not much else.

Procedure

Class work leading to pair work.

Pre-test
First of all, test how many words each learner can remember out of 16. Ask the class to call out 16 names of objects very slowly. Tell all the learners to write down every word and to try to remember them. Then tell them to cover their list and write down as many of the words as they can remember. Finally, checking against their list, they note down the number they remembered. You should also try to remember them, making use of your system. If you have mastered your system you should remember all 16. The learners, on the other hand, will probably remember between five and eight of them. Declare your own result and wait for the admiration and praise to subside a little! Then ask the class to give you, alone, 16 words to remember. All the learners should write down the list and number the words. This gives *them* practice and *you* time to fix the words to your usual system! They will be amazed that you can remember all the words *and* that you can remember the words both in and out of sequence, according to number.

The learners should copy your memory-system objects and spend a few minutes trying to learn them. They should test each other.

Post-test
Each learner should write out 16 more names of objects and use these to test their neighbour's mastery of the system. This achievement in the post-test may then be compared with that of the pre-test. From the point of view of a language teacher, this is a game offering considerable potential, particularly once you have taught the memory trick. Then the learners can explain *their* bizarre memory pictures, for example, 'Number 11 was the President and I saw spaghetti wrapped all around him.'

Magic tricks

Language can sometimes be exemplified in a concise and memorable way through a magic trick. Furthermore, it is normal to *practise* a magic trick in order to master it. From the point of view of language learning, this is marvellous! There is an authentic need for repetition.

Because magic tricks always attract attention and invite comment, there is a potentially large occurrence of other language – the hidden language of the game.

In short, magic tricks, although apparently frivolous, have a serious role in language learning.

But who is going to do the magic trick? You may well feel reluctant to take on the role of magician. If this is the case, you might like to explain the trick before the lesson to a competent learner who can then do the performance for you. If the trick fails or seems very naive – all the better. The learners can show you how to do it more skilfully.

20   Kaboom

Language	Describing actions, both in the past (*I picked up the coin*) and in the future (*I'm going to pick up the coin*). The negative is used in both (*I didn't pick up . . .* and *I'm not going to pick up . . .*).
Skills	Listening and speaking.
Control	Controlled.
Level	Beginners. This trick has obvious appeal to young learners. However, older people might like to learn it in order to try it out on their children or younger brothers or sisters.
Time	2–3 minutes to demonstrate the trick. 20 minutes for all learners to learn the trick in pair work.
Materials	You need a small, flat object, for example, a coin or a small piece of paper. You also need a bigger object to cover the smaller one, for example, a book or a plate.

Magic tricks

Preparation

Collect the necessary objects.

Procedure

Class work leading to pair work.

Hold up the small object so that all the class can identify it. Put it on the table. Hold up the larger object also for identification. Put the larger object on top of the smaller object. Then say:

I'm going to pick up the (coin).
But I'm not going to pick up the (book).
Kaboom!

Invite a learner to come to the desk and to look underneath the big object. As the learner does so, pick up the small object. Then say:

I picked up the (coin).
But I didn't pick up the (book).
You did!

Ask the learners if they would like to learn the trick to try out on others.

Get a number of them to try the trick out in front of the class. When you are confident that everyone has learned the words and actions, ask them to practise it in pairs.

It helps the transition to pair work if you write the sentences on the board as above.

Warning: Choose someone to look underneath the (book) who is not too much of a sceptic! He/she might refuse. Say to him/her encouragingly, 'Have a look!'

21   The matchbox

Language	Asking questions and making statements, with use of *some* and *any*.
Skills	Listening and speaking.
Control	Controlled.
Level	Beginners.
Time	3–5 minutes to do the trick. 20 minutes for all learners to learn the trick.
Materials	Matchboxes and matches; rubber band.

Preparation

You need two matchboxes. One of them should be half full of matches and placed inside your right sleeve. You may have to fasten it to your forearm with a rubber band. The other box, also half full of matches, should be on the table in front of you.

For pair work you will need the same materials for each pair. If this proves difficult, then you will only be able to let a few learners try the trick.

Procedure

Class work leading to pair work.

Hold up the box on the table and shake it.

Teacher: Are there any matches in the box?

Class: Yes.

Teacher: (*Pointing at one learner.*) Do you think there are any matches in the box?

Learner: Yes.

Teacher: (*Open the box and take the matches out.*) Are there any matches in the box now?

Class: No!

Teacher: (*Shake the closed box with your left hand.*) Are there any matches in it now?

Class: No!

Teacher: (*Shake the box with your right hand. There will seem to be matches in it because the ones inside your sleeve will be rattling!*) Are there any matches in it?

Class: No! . . . Yes!
Teacher: (*Open the box in your hand.*) Are there any matches in it?
Class: No (there aren't).
Teacher: (*Now shake it first with your left then with your right hand.
           Ask the question each time. Finally the learners will realise
           that you have a matchbox up your sleeve. Reveal it and
           remove it.*) Are there any matches in *this* box?
Class: Yes!
Teacher: (*Open the box and show the matches.*) Yes, there are some
           matches in it!
           (*Show the empty box.*) There aren't any matches in this box.
           But there are some in this one.

Show one or two learners how to do the trick and what to say.
Then organise the activity as pair work. It would be helpful if
you put the following sentences on the board:

Are there any . . . in this box?
Yes, there are.
No, there aren't.
There aren't any . . . but there are some . . .

22   Climbing through a postcard

Language	Talking about the action of climbing through a postcard, using *going to* (*I'm going to climb through it*), and the present perfect (*I've climbed through it*).
Skills	Listening and speaking.
Control	Controlled.
Level	Beginners/intermediate.
Time	2–3 minutes to demonstrate the trick. 20 minutes for all learners to prepare their card and climb through it.
Materials	You need one postcard or a plain piece of card of postcard size or larger for yourself, and a pair of scissors. Have enough card or paper for each learner as well.

Preparation

Collect the necessary materials. It is advisable to practise the trick
beforehand at home!

Procedure

Class work leading to pair work.

Ask if anyone can climb through the piece of card. Ask if *they* think
you can. Now cut the card as shown in the diagram.

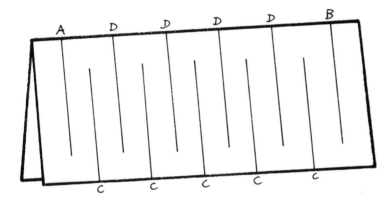

1 Fold it in half lengthways.
2 Make two cuts A, B.
3 Cut along fold from A to B.
4 Now do alternate cuts C, D, C, D, etc., cutting through *both* halves of
   the folded card.

As you prepare the card say:

Teacher: I'm going to cut the card. ·
          I'm cutting the card.
          I've cut the card.

Now shake out the zigzag circle of card and climb through it, not
forgetting to say:

Teacher: I'm going to climb through it.
          I'm climbing through it.
          I've climbed through it.

If you *don't* want to climb through it, ask a learner to go through it for
you. You can then introduce, 'He's going to . . .' etc.

Organise pair work in the usual way, making sure that everyone
knows how to cut the card.

Write the six sentences on the board.

Suggest that the trick is well practised so that it can be demonstrated to friends or other classes without fault. And this means frequent repetition of the language!

23 The piece of string

Language	Talking about a trick, using *going to* (*I'm going to cut* . . .), the present continuous (*I'm cutting* . . .), and the present perfect (*I've mended it*).
Skills	Listening, speaking and reading.
Control	Controlled.
Level	Beginners/intermediate.
Time	2–3 minutes to demonstrate the trick. 20 minutes for all learners to learn the trick in pair work.
Materials	You need a piece of string about 20 cm long and another piece *of the same type* about 8 cm long. You also need a pair of scissors. Each pair of learners will also have to be equipped in the same way if they are to practise the trick.

Preparation

Collect the necessary materials. It is advisable to practise the trick beforehand at home!

Procedure

Class work leading to pair work.

Before the class begins, fold the smaller piece of string in half and keep it in your hand. (The hand you do *not* use for scissors!) At the beginning of the trick take up the longer piece of string, fold it in half and place it next to the other.

Then, with the point of your scissors raise the bend of the *shorter* piece of string and slowly cut it.

Then scramble *all* the string into your hand and say you are mending it.

Then take one end of the long piece of string and pull it sharply, claiming that it has been mended. As your arm surges upwards, drawing people's attention in that direction, drop the two little pieces of cut string on the floor.

Teacher: I'm going to cut this piece of string. (*Hold the string up.*)

I'm cutting it. (*Cut the short piece of string.*)

I've cut it. (*Indicate the cut ends.*)

Now . . .

I'm going to mend it. (*Put all string in hand.*)

I'm mending it. (*Squeeze it and look magical.*)

I've mended it. (*Pull out long piece of string, drop short piece.*)

Of course, someone will eventually notice the pieces of string on the floor. Then you can offer to teach the trick to them.

For pair work it would be advisable to demonstrate the trick with one or two learners to ensure that the sequence of events is understood.

Write the six sentences on the board.

After some practice, you might remove the sentences from the board.

Keep the small piece of string folded in your hand. Don't let the class see it!

Place the long piece of string next to the short one. The class see the other side of your hand.

short piece!

long piece!

Pull up the short piece of string with the scissors. The class think it is the long piece.

When you have put all the string into your hand pull up the end of the long piece. Then say your magic words... pull it upwards. Amazing!

24   Magic birthday

Language	Language of simple arithmetic.
Skills	Listening and speaking.
Control	Controlled.
Level	Beginners.
Time	10 minutes
Materials	Chalkboard.

Preparation

None.

Procedure

Class work leading to pair work.

There are many examples of magic with numbers. This is just one example and involves birthdays, which gives it an extra usefulness for the language teacher.

Ask a learner to multiply his age by three, add six and divide by three. Then he must subtract two from the result. The answer will be – the age of the learner! Having amazed everyone, write the process on the board and ask the learners to work with their neighbour, trying out a number of different ages.

25   Nine-square mind-reading trick

Language	Asking questions beginning with *Is . . . ?*
Skills	Listening and speaking.
Control	Controlled.
Level	Beginners.
Time	A few minutes each time you do the trick.
Materials	Chalkboard or OHP.

Preparation

You need an assistant. (We like to choose learners who do not usually achieve very much in the language classroom!) Teach your assistant the very simple trick (see the end of *Procedure*).

Draw (or project) nine rectangles, like those in the illustration. In this version there are nine pictures of a stickman doing different things.

Procedure

Class work leading to group work.

Ask who believes in telepathy. Discuss it in the mother tongue. Raise the fun and involvement in the idea through encouraging disagreement.

Then ask your assistant to go out of the room. Ask the class to choose one of the rectangles, for example, the 'man running' and to concentrate on it. Ask your assistant to come into the room. Say that everyone is thinking of what the stickman is doing. Then, pointing to the pictures, ask your assistant:

Teacher: Is he running?
Learner: No.
Teacher: Is he reading?
Learner: No.
Teacher: Is he swimming?
Learner: Yes.

Your assistant will know which it is by the way you point! Here's the trick:

The class have chosen the *top right-hand corner* of the big rectangle. So you *point* to the *top right-hand corner* of the first picture you ask a question about, i.e. where we have put a little cross on the diagram. With your first pointing, your assistant knows which picture has been chosen! It does not matter which picture you point to first.

If you would like to really amaze the class, agree on a different trick with your assistant!

Instead of pointing, place a piece of chalk casually on a book in a position equivalent to the position of the picture chosen by the class. So the swimming picture would be represented as in the illustration.

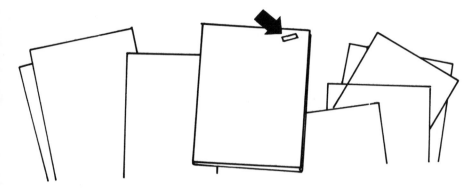

Your assistant enters the room, sees the chalk and immediately knows which picture it is. The class can call out the questions. You do not even need to be in the room!

Variation
Class work
   Instead of stickmen, you can show clock time, objects or a short text in each rectangle.

Note: We suggest you only do this game a few times and that you and your assistant keep the secret for months! It does not provide a lot of opportunity for language use but it does not take much time either. It is an immense source of interest and goodwill!

26   Black mind-reading trick

Language	Questions beginning with *Is it . . . ?*
Skills	Listening and speaking.
Control	Guided.
Level	Beginners/intermediate.
Time	5 minutes for class work; 20 minutes for group work.
Materials	None.

Preparation

You need an assistant. Before the lesson, tell your assistant that he/she will be asked to leave the room. The class will then choose an object in the classroom. You will then call your assistant inside and ask questions (see *Procedure*) to find out whether he/she realises which object you and the class are thinking about. Your assistant will know which object it is because you will refer to a black object *before* the chosen object.

Procedure

Class work leading to group work.

   (This game will amaze the class if it follows on from the serious trial of telepathy described in Game 11.)

   The 'telepath' (you) stays in the room. The 'telepath's' accomplice goes out of the room. The class choose an object and think about it. The accomplice re-enters the room. The 'telepath' (you) then asks questions, e.g.

'Telepath': Is it the cupboard?
Accomplice: No.
'Telepath': Is it the English poster?
Accomplice: No.
'Telepath': Is it John's nose?
Accomplice: No.

At one point the 'telepath' will point to a black object. *The accomplice will know that the chosen object is the next one.*

'Telepath': Is it this black pen?
Accomplice: No.
'Telepath': Is it Sandra's bag?
Accomplice: Yes.

Up to now the class has listened to you and to your accomplice. Hopefully they have been impressed! Play the game twice, each time asking the class to guess how you are doing the trick. If they do not find out by themselves, tell them.

   Now is the time for the class to devise new versions of the same trick. Divide the class into small groups and say that each group must decide on its own trick. The trick in each case must be based on words. (For example, the answer follows the first use of: a possessive form; a preposition; an adjective of size or perhaps of texture; *this* or *that*; *Do you think it's the . . .?* an exclamation, e.g. *Oh dear, what next . . .?* or *Now . . .*, or *What next, I know, what about . . .?*)Each group should then try out their trick in the class and see if the others can discover the secret verbal signal!

Caring and sharing games

Our ideas for this section derive, in part, from the work of G. Moskowitz and, in part, from the experience of youth club and community leaders.

All the games in this section demand and encourage trust and interest in others. We believe these values are native to everyone. However, in some cultures they may not be associated with school or college and with foreign-language learning. You may for this reason have some difficulty in overcoming your learners' shyness or reluctance to share personal feelings and experiences with other class members. Only you can decide how and when to make the attempt to introduce the learners to caring and sharing activities, but we believe the following points to be generally true:

1 The teacher must believe – and be seen to believe – in the value of the learners coming to understand each other in the English lesson and through the medium of English. Most learners want to learn English not only to exchange impersonal information (buy tickets, ask the way, etc.) but also to get to know people. It is essential, therefore, that English is used for that purpose by the learners in the classroom.

    We also believe in the value of people getting to know each other and learning to respect and value others whenever it is possible. And clearly language-learning lessons offer the opportunity for this kind of development.

2 The teacher and the class must be convinced that the language used in the caring and sharing activities is relevant to 'real life' situations, i.e. situations out of school where English is used.

3 Learners are more likely to accept caring and sharing activities – this applies to *all* games, group work, etc. – if they are introduced to these activities in the early years of foreign-language learning.

27   A remembering-names game

Language	Names of people in the class.
Skills	Listening and speaking.
Control	Controlled.
Level	Beginners.
Time	10 minutes.
Materials	A screwed-up ball of paper for each group.

Preparation

Prepare the balls of paper.

Procedure

Group work, or class work for small classes.

This game is intended for learners who do not know each other very well. It is one of the many games which help people in a group to learn each other's names quickly. Arrange the learners in a circle. (There should not be more than 12 or 15 in a circle, so more circles if necessary!) Give one learner a tight ball of paper. He/she must then throw it to anyone else in the circle. The learner catching the ball must say his/her own name before throwing the ball to someone else. After everyone has said their name at least twice, you change the rules. Now the thrower must say the name of the person they are going to throw the ball to.

If the catcher misses the ball or drops it the *thrower* must retrieve the ball, return to his/her place, and then choose someone else to throw the ball to. And so it continues.

Variation
Group or class work.

You can alter the rules by asking players not to throw the ball to the same person twice or by insisting that the ball is only thrown to someone of the opposite sex.

28   Getting to know each other

Language	Questions and answers about personal characteristics.
Skills	Listening and speaking, with some reading and writing.
Control	Guided.
Level	All.
Time	15–20 minutes (depending on the level).
Materials	One card 100 mm × 150 mm for each learner. Chalkboard or OHP.

Preparation

Collect or cut enough cards for the class.

Procedure

Class work.

The basis of this activity and its variations is 'question and answer'. The nature of caring and sharing games, however, is that the learners concentrate on their experiences, opinions and feelings rather than on a general exchange of more material information.

With the help of the learners, make a list on the board or OHP of the personal details people often like to know about each other, for example, favourite music, favourite famous person, dislikes, material possessions, most frightening thing . . .

Give each learner a card about 100 mm × 150 mm and ask them to write:
a) their name on it in letters at least 10 mm high
b) four *categories* of personal detail they would not mind telling people about

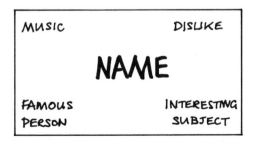

Then help the learners to fasten these cards to their clothes. If this is not possible, they should hold their card so that other people can see it. All the learners should circulate around the room looking at each other's names and perhaps greeting each other. When you say 'Stop!' (or turn off music which you might have been playing), each learner should then enter into conversation with the nearest person. Each learner should ask the other about the personal information indicated on the card.

The learners should not merely name, for example, the person who is so important in their life but be asked to say why, perhaps to give examples, etc. After a few minutes ask the learners to continue to circulate (perhaps by starting up the music again) until you stop them once more. Each learner should talk with about five others.

At the end you might ask who found people who like or dislike the same things, have the same aims or similar heroes, etc.

Variation
Class work.

In this version the theme is finding what people have in common rather than a more general exchange of information.

Each person writes on a sticky label their first name, their family name, their favourite colour and their favourite hobby (or they could use cards, as in the main game). The sticky label is stuck on to their clothes and then everyone wanders about the room until they find someone with whom they share something according to the label. Through conversation each learner tries to find as many things in common with their partner as possible: likes, dislikes, possessions, fears, ambitions, prejudices, etc.

This information should not be shared in general terms with the class as a whole. However, you might invite people to relate any surprising discoveries and coincidences if they are happy to do so. For example:

John and I have motorcycles and we both like photography.
I met Peter Franklin. He and I both like Nadine Gordimer's novels and we have both been to Italy for our holidays.
Mrs Whitecross and I both smoke and wish we didn't and we both think we should take more exercise.

29   Guess who it is

Language	Making statements about self.
Skills	Principally listening and speaking.
Control	Guided.
Level	Intermediate/advanced.
Time	30–40 minutes. It depends how many learners speak!
Materials	Paper and pencils and a box or other container.

Preparation

None.

Procedure

Class or group work.

The learners should know each other quite well. Each learner writes his/her name on a piece of paper. The names are then put into a box and mixed together. Then each learner takes a name from the box at random. After ten minutes' preparation, each learner speaks as if he/she was the person named on the paper. They talk about their character, interests, likes and dislikes, habits, etc. For example:

I am very quiet.
I like the English lesson although I never speak!
I often eat my sandwich during the lesson!

The class or group decide who the person is.

Variation
Group work.

Have an even number of groups, as each group must work with another. Each group chooses one person in the other group to talk about without letting anyone in the other group overhear. *The aim is to pack a suitcase for the person they have chosen.* Each item must be carefully chosen to convey the person's character, habits and needs.

Then groups take it in turns to read out their list of objects to pack. The other group has to say who they think the suitcase has been packed for. Then they discuss whether it was a sensible choice in all respects, and, of course, the person chosen will no doubt have some opinions!

30 Truth, dare and promise

Language	Questions and commands.
Skills	All the skills, principally listening and speaking.
Control	Guided.
Level	Beginners/intermediate.
Time	If the writing is done for homework then allow approximately 20–30 minutes.
Materials	A piece of card for each learner.

Preparation

You might like to prepare examples of sentences which you know the learners can compose. This will give them an idea of what you want.

Procedure

Individual work leading to group work.

This game is intended for learners who know each other well and have an informal relationship. It is probably best to set the writing for homework before the oral work. Each learner should write one or two sentences on a card for each of the three categories below. Before using the sentences in oral work it would be wise to check that each 'truth', 'dare', or 'promise' is acceptable to you. Here are the categories and some sample sentences:

Truth
Is it true that you are often anxious?
Is it true that you go to a lot of parties?
Is it true that you don't like classical music?

Dare
I dare you to pretend that you are a bee.
I dare you to sing a song.

Promise
Promise to shake everybody by the hand at the end of the lesson.
Promise to draw your self-portrait on the board.

Each group should place all their cards in a pile upside down. Each learner takes it in turns to pick up a card. Before doing so he/she must choose which one of the three categories to take, 'truth', 'dare', or 'promise'. They then look at the card and read out the sentence in the category they have chosen! Then they must do what the card demands!

31 Six eyes

Language	Making statements about people, using present simple verbs and adverbs of frequency, e.g. *often, usually, always*.
Skills	All.
Control	Guided.
Level	Intermediate/advanced.
Time	30 minutes.
Materials	A piece of paper for each learner.

Preparation

None.

Procedure

Group work.
   The learners should know each other quite well. Each learner writes his/her name on a small piece of paper. These are then folded and jumbled. Each learner then takes one of the pieces of paper and tries to imagine that they *are* that person. They must then complete the following sentences:

I always (enjoy reading a good book).
I often (study and think about things).
I usually (go to work by car).
I occasionally (go to England).
I rarely (eat kippers).
I never (ride on camels).

Then everyone tries to guess who the learner has pretended to be. The learner who has been represented by those sentences should then have an opportunity to comment!

32 Questionnaires

Language	The language of the questionnaire which you devise, plus the language of the responses to the questions.
Skills	All the skills, principally listening and speaking.
Control	Guided.
Level	All.
Time	20–30 minutes, depending on the length of the questionnaire.
Materials	Paper and pencils/pens; for Variation 1, chalkboard or OHP (optional).

Preparation

You could prepare the questionnaire yourself. However, it would perhaps be more significant socially and in terms of language learning if the questionnaire was devised by you and the class working together.

Procedure

Pair work leading to group or class work.

This game is best played by people who know each other quite well. Initially the learners work in pairs, each establishing information about his/her partner by means of a questionnaire. In one version of the activity, the information might be chiefly physical and related to basic likes and dislikes. In another, the information might be more personal and border on the private. The teacher must judge whether the latter is appropriate.

The completed questionnaires are then displayed on the classroom walls or on tables. Ask a learner to choose one at random and read out the information. The class (with the exception of the two learners concerned) must try to decide who the information is about.

Variation 1
Group or class work.

The learners should know each other quite well. You ask a series of questions. You might ask them orally or write them on the board or OHP. The learners must write down their answers very rapidly, incorporating the gist of the question in their answer. Although grammatical accuracy is important in this activity, the idea the learner wishes to convey is the main concern, e.g.

What would you do if you found a lot of money in a park?
If I found a lot of money in a park I would keep some of it and take the
    rest of it to the police!

When you have asked about five questions, collect in the papers and then read out each one. The class must listen and decide who wrote each set of answers.

Variation 2
Pair work.
    Each learner writes ten questions which he/she feels would be revealing of their own personality, interests and concerns if put to them.
    Organise the class into pairs. The learners ask their partners the questions they had written for themselves to answer, e.g.

What is your greatest fear?
What is your favourite type of holiday?

Variation 3
Pair work.
    Each learner devises ten questions and writes them down. Then he/she writes the answers he/she would expect their partner to give. *Then* they put the questions and compare the answers.

33 Fortune-telling

Language	Predicting future events, using *will* and *going to*.
Skills	All.
Control	Free.
Level	All.
Time	30 minutes.
Materials	Paper and pencils/pens.

Preparation

None.

Procedure

Group work.

The learners need not know each other well. People love having their fortunes told, even if the prediction is clearly without any foundation! There are a number of ways of organising this activity. Essentially, however, each learner writes a fortune for someone else.

One version goes as follows: in a group of four or five learners each learner writes a fortune or prediction for each of the others. In other words each learner writes four or five fortunes. Then, in turn, each learner is given all his/her fortunes. He/she must read them out and comment, for example, on whether some of them are the same, or just what he/she had hoped for, or highly unlikely.

34 Personal opinions

Language	Making statements about people and one's attitudes towards them. Reported speech.
Skills	All.
Control	Free.
Level	All.
Time	30 minutes.
Materials	Several cards or small pieces of paper for each learner.

Preparation

None.

Procedure

Group or class work.

The learners should know and like each other. Each learner prepares a number of cards or small pieces of paper. Each card should have one sentence on it which describes a person. You may have to help them to get the sentences right! The sentences may be complimentary or critical. Obviously the ideas and the language should be appropriate to the cultural beliefs, the individual personality and the language proficiency of the class. Having said that, here are some examples:

You've got a thoughtful face.
You look very intelligent.
Your hair is beautiful.
You look rather sad.
You are very kind.
You look aggressive.
You are aggressive.
You are not very friendly.
You always think that you are right.
You never admit that you can be wrong.
I'd like to go on holiday with you.
I'd like to be stuck in an elevator (lift) with you.
I wouldn't like to be stuck in an elevator (lift) with you.
You look like a hard person but really you are kind and gentle.
You look quite innocent but really you are a bit of a devil.
You have probably broken the hearts of hundreds of women/men.

When the cards are ready, collect them into a pile. Ask a volunteer to take a card, to read it *silently* and to give it to the person he/she feels it describes.

The person receiving the card must read out the sentence, changing the wording only to repeat it as the other person's opinion, e.g. 'June thinks that I am the ugliest person in the class!' The receiver and anybody else in the group can respond immediately, agreeing with the opinion or rejecting it. Some opinions lead to discussion rather than to the simple exchange of statement of agreement or disagreement.

35   Reading someone's mind

Language	Making statements about other people, using the phrase *I think you are* . . . and adjectives.
Skills	Listening and speaking.
Control	Free.
Level	Intermediate/advanced.
Time	10–15 minutes.
Materials	None.

Preparation

None.

Procedure

Class work.

If possible, arrange the class in two circles, one standing inside the other. Each learner should face someone in the other circle. If it is not possible to organise the class in this way the learners should be able to circulate freely and should begin by facing one other person.

Tell the learners that quiet and responsive concentration on another person can often produce a sensation of what they are like, what they are feeling. Ask them to be very quiet and to face their partner and to concentrate *on them* for a few moments. After half a minute or so ask them to tell each other what it was they felt and understood about the other person. If they were *not* thinking about them at all they must say what they *were* thinking about!

Note: Before starting this activity you could discuss with the learners the sort of feelings one can sense in other people and you could make sure they have the language to express these understandings:

I think you are . . .
rather, a little, very, extremely . . .
    happy, anxious, worried, angry, frustrated, irritable, cheerful,
    generous, careful, cautious, friendly, reserved, funny, serious,
    thoughtful, kind, mean, self-centred, open-hearted . . .

Card and board games

We have included in this section adaptations of several well-known and well-bred card games and board games. *Snakes and ladders* and *Happy families* appear under their usual titles. A map game (*Search*) is included and also an adaptation and extension of the gift game (*Presents, and rewards and punishments*).

We believe that the learners will enjoy and derive value from the basic games we have described here. However, in order for the full value of this section to be achieved, it is essential for the learners to help you invent and make variations. Suggestions about how to organise this creative contribution are given where appropriate.

36   Snakes and ladders

Language	Counting, in the main game; reading and responding to written instructions in Variations 1 and 2; in addition, in Variation 2, learners must write instructions for others.
Skills	Reading and speaking; also, in Variation 2, writing.
Control	Controlled in the main game and Variation 1; guided or free in Variation 2.
Level	Beginners for the main game; beginners or intermediate for the variations.
Time	Depends on the size of the board used.
Materials	Large pieces of stiff card, counters and a die (see *Preparation*).

Preparation

For the main game (counting), you need a grid or a track, made up of interconnected squares, all numbered, extending from 1 to 100 – or, for a quicker game, a number less than 100. Every so often along the way, draw a ladder (which has its base in one square, and its top in a square much further *on* in the number sequence); also, every so often along the way, draw a snake (with its head in one square and its tail in a square much further *back* in the number sequence).

For Variation 1, you will need to write instructions on certain squares, e.g. 'Go back three squares'. Alternatively, you may prefer to write instructions on a set of 'chance' cards (see below).

For Variation 2, the learners will write instructions (see below).

When making the grid or track, you should use fairly thick card, and always store it flat. Should it curl, playing the game becomes difficult, since the players' counters, which are used to mark their progress along the number sequence, may slip and slide off. Instead of measuring and ruling the squares on the card, you may find it easier to cut the desired number of squares from a sheet of card, write all numbers and instructions on them first, and then stick them down on a second sheet of card. This way, any mistakes can be corrected as you work, by taking a fresh square of card; and, later on, when the game has lost its novelty, fresh instructions can be substituted for the old ones, since the latter can be prised or torn loose.

Procedure

Pair work, or small groups.

In the standard version of *Snakes and ladders*, the players take it in turns to throw the die and move their counter ahead along a numbered track or grid. They move the same number of squares along the track or grid as the number thrown on the die. Their aim is to be the first to reach 'Home' at the far end of the number sequence. Landing on a snake's head along the way means that a player must go back to the square containing the snake's tail. Landing at the foot of a ladder takes a player up and on to the square containing the top of the ladder. As they move their counters, the players must count the moves out loud.

Variation 1
Pair work, or small groups.

Language practice (beyond counting) can be worked into *Snakes and ladders* by writing various instructions into every third or fourth or fifth square, e.g. 'Go back three squares' or 'Go forward four squares' or 'Miss a turn'.

Instead of writing the instructions directly into the squares on the grid or track, since the size of the squares limits the length of the instructions, you may prefer to write them on separate cards, cut to whatever size you please. These 'chance' cards, as they are called, should be shuffled and placed face down in a pile before the game is started. Players are directed to 'Take a chance card' by a written instruction to that effect written directly on the grid or track. They should take the topmost card. The instructions on the 'chance' cards can represent good luck, sending the players forward along the number sequence, or they can represent bad luck, sending them back. 'Reasons' for the good or bad luck may be given, perhaps drawing on the language and content of a story book or textbook studied by the class, e.g. 'Your alarm clock does not go off. Miss a turn'; or 'You are given a lift in a friend's car. Go forward three squares.'

Variation 2
Pair work, or small groups.

Instead of writing the instructions for the game yourself, ask the learners to write 'chance' cards, either in class or for homework, for others to use when playing the game. As in Variation 1, it may be a good idea to draw the content and language of the instructions from a story book or textbook.

37 Happy families

Language	Making requests; revision of vocabulary.
Skills	Listening and speaking; also, in the variation, reading.
Control	Controlled.
Level	Beginners/intermediate.
Time	At least 5 minutes.
Materials	Pictures and pieces of card (see *Preparation*).

Preparation

For each group of players, you will need a set of 36 small pictures, all mounted on pieces of card which are the same size. These pictures must be carefully selected so that they fall into nine clearly distinguishable 'families', i.e. four pictures constitute a family. The distinguishing feature may be, for example, a common name, as in the traditional game in which we find Mr Bun, the baker; his wife, Mrs Bun; and his children, Master and Miss Bun. But the game is adaptable, so we could have families of objects or clothes or items of food, all of different colour or size. It is important that you select only pictures for which the learners already know the language, and that you tell them before the game starts what the families are, and how the members of each family are to be identified.

Procedure

Group work.

This is a game for four players. One player (the dealer) shares out the picture cards, shuffling the set first, and dealing them out face down so that no one sees the others' cards. Each player looks at his/her own cards and sorts them out into as many complete families as there are. (There may be none!) All complete families are placed face down in front of each player.

The players take it in turns to ask one other player for any card that is needed to make up an incomplete family. If the player who is asked has the card in question, he/she must hand it over. As before, when a family is completed, the cards are placed face down in front of the player to whom they belong. The first player to complete all his/her families is the winner.

Direct the learners to use an appropriate (and polite) form of words when asking for cards, and when replying to each other, e.g.

Learner 1: Have you got . . . please?
        or: I'm looking for . . .
        or: I would like . . .
Learner 2: Yes. Here you are.
        or: No. I'm sorry.
Learner 1 (if answer is 'Yes'): Thanks.
        or (if answer is 'No'): O.K. I'll ask someone else next time.

Players who forget to say 'Please' should miss a turn!

Variation
Group work.

Instead of using picture cards for the game, you may write the names of families of objects on the cards. (This is quicker to prepare, but less attractive to use, perhaps, and requires the learners to read rather than recall the vocabulary items being revised.) However, the written form of the game is ideal if you want to focus the learners' attention on certain formal characteristics of words, e.g. rhyming words. Here, you should write one example from a family in the centre of a card, with the other three members of the family in the corner. (See illustration.)

```
┌─────────────────┐        ┌─────────────────┐
│                 │        │                 │
│  through        │        │  plough         │
│                 │        │                 │
│                 │        │                 │
│  glue           │        │  now            │
│  zoo            │        │  bough          │
│  two            │        │  cow            │
│                 │        │                 │
└─────────────────┘        └─────────────────┘
```

38   Search

Language	Simple questions and answers (answers taken from written cards); giving map references; also, in the variation, writing short sentences.
Skills	All.
Control	Controlled or guided, in the main game; in the variation, learners write sentences, which can be guided or free.
Level	Intermediate.
Time	At least 15 minutes.
Materials	For each pair of learners you will need two identical maps, a set of cards and a coin or token. (See *Preparation*).

Preparation

Draw two identical outline maps. The maps should be simple, showing (for example) an island with mountain, forest, river, lake and town. The maps should be divided up into squares, so that locations can be given by grid references. The references from West to East – i.e. from left to right of the map, assuming that North is to the top – should be given by letters of the alphabet, as many letters as there are squares. The references from South to North – i.e. bottom to top – should be by numbers. Thus, different squares on the map can be referred to as A1, B5, G10, etc.

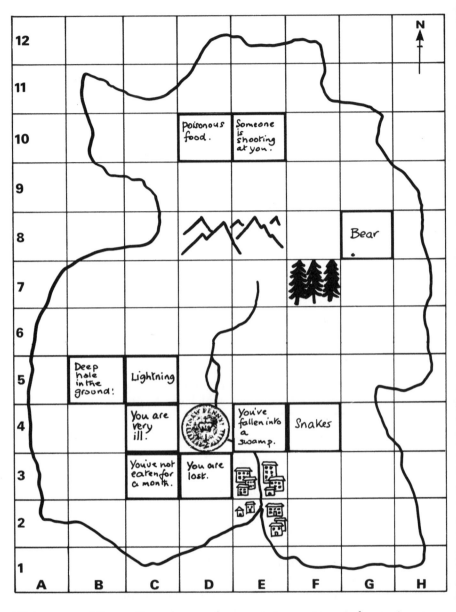

Write a set of 'hazard' cards – cards containing written information about danger and bad luck that might be encountered in the place shown on the map, e.g. swamps, poisonous snakes, illness, shortage of food. Each card should be of a size to fit exactly into any of the squares on the map. The players will also need a coin or token to show 'treasure', or whatever other goal is decided on for the game.

Procedure

Pair work.

One player secretly adds a specified number of hazards to a map. The other player, who has an identical copy of the map, first tries to find out by questioning where at least some of the hazards are, then moves about the area shown on the map, searching for treasure, or some other goal. He/she has a certain number of 'lives', i.e. can survive so many accidental encounters with hazards. The object of the game is to find the treasure, or whatever, before all one's 'lives' have been used up.

Example

Give one copy of a prepared outline map of an island to one player. It is his/her job to select ten 'hazard' cards from a collection of such cards provided by you. You may control the language by spelling out the hazards in full, e.g. 'You've fallen into a swamp.' If you prefer, you may simply state a key word or phrase, e.g. 'jungle' or 'poisonous snakes', in which case the learners must expand them into full sentences for themselves when playing the game, as described below.

The first player places the selected ten cards wherever he/she likes on the map, making sure that the other player does not see. A cardboard screen or book can be used to hide the map and cards.

Once the ten cards are in position, the second player asks the first player five questions, no more, about what might be contained in five specified squares, e.g.

Learner 1: What's in square A3?
   or: Is there anything dangerous in square A3?
The first player must answer truthfully, e.g.
Learner 2: A swamp.
   or: There's nothing there.
      etc.

The second player should fill in his/her own copy of the map with the location of any hazard that is discovered by asking the five questions.

Now the first player should secretly place a coin or token on his/her copy of the map, to indicate the location of a hoard of treasure. This done, the 'explorer' i.e. the second player, is ready to begin his/her search of the island.

The second player decides whereabouts on the coastline of the island to start, and then moves from there, referring to his/her own copy of the map and calling out the grid references for each stage of the journey.

Note: The explorer may move only one square at a time; vertical, horizontal and diagonal moves are all allowed. He/she should, of

course, avoid all those squares already marked as containing hazards.
Thus:

Learner 2: B7.
    or: I'm moving to square B7.

Should the second player accidentally make a move into a square that
contains a hazard – i.e. a hazard of which he/she had no prior
knowledge – then the first player must call out the bad news, e.g.

Learner 1: You've fallen into a river.

(The nature of the hazard is spelled out in full on the card, or briefly
indicated, as described above.)

    For each hazard that the second player encounters, one 'life' from a
total of five 'lives' is lost. If the player succeeds in finding the square that
contains the treasure before all five 'lives' have been lost, then he/she
has won the game.

Variation
Pair work.

    Instead of writing the 'hazard' cards yourself, ask pairs of learners to
do so for others to play with. The setting for the game (i.e. the map) and
the hazards may be derived, perhaps, from a story that you are reading
together in class.

39 Presents, and rewards and punishments

Language	Discussion, justifying and challenging choices; also, in Variation 2, describing people.
Skills	Listening and speaking; also, in Variation 2, reading and writing.
Control	Free.
Level	Advanced.
Time	At least 20 minutes.
Materials	Sets of cards (see *Preparation*).

Preparation

Make a set of 'person' cards, at least one per player, but preferably with some extra. Each 'person' card should contain a picture of a person, with a brief written description below, e.g. 'Uncle, retired teacher, likes fishing and reading.' Also make a set of 'present' cards, at least three times as many as you have 'person' cards. Each 'present' card should contain either a picture of something which might conceivably be given as a present, or a brief written description of such an object,' e.g. book of poems, bottle of whisky, fishing rod, record of Country and Western music, bicycle. For Variation 3, you will need to make sets of 'reward' cards and 'punishment' cards, instead of 'present' cards.

Procedure

Group work.

Players take a 'person' card, either randomly from the shuffled set of 'person' cards, or deliberately choosing someone for whom they would like to find suitable presents.

The first player takes the top card from the set of 'present' cards. (These should be shuffled and placed in a pile, face down.) *Whatever card happens to be topmost, the player must attempt to justify giving it to his/her own particular person.* This may or may not be easy! For example, it would obviously be easy to justify giving a fishing rod to the uncle who likes fishing, but less easy to justify giving a skateboard. This would be easier to justify as a present for a teenage cousin, for example. If the other players in the group agree that a good case has been put up for a particular present, then the same player takes another card from the pile of 'present' cards, and continues in similar fashion until the vote goes against him/her. Then it is the turn of the next player to take a card from the pile and justify giving that present to his/her own person. Play proceeds either until all cards have been used, or until a predetermined time limit has been reached – perhaps 25 minutes. The player with most presents for his/her person wins.

Variation 1
Group work.

A 'non-random' version of the game may be played in which all the 'present' cards are spread out, *not* put in a pile. They should be placed face down, in neat rows and columns. Each player may examine one, two or three cards before choosing the one that seems most appropriate for his/her own person i.e. the one that will be easiest to justify giving as a present. Pictures which the player decides not to choose must be returned face down to their original position, but not before all the players have had a chance to see them. The player must also say why it is not an acceptable present. This version of the game reduces the likelihood of having to attempt to justify bizarre choices of presents, at least in the opening rounds of the game, but increases the need for the players to pay close attention to *all* the cards played throughout the game, as in Pelmanism.

Variation 2
Group work.

Instead of providing the learners with ready-made 'person' cards, i.e. cards that contain both a picture of a person and a written description, you may prefer to provide them with pictures only. It is then for the learners to write their own descriptions of the persons shown in the pictures. This they should do on slips of paper that are affixed to the picture cards with paper clips. After the game, the written descriptions can be removed, so that fresh descriptions can be written for the pictures when the game is next played, perhaps by different learners.

Variation 3
Group work.

Great fun can be had from a version of the game in which rewards and/or punishments are given to famous (or infamous) people. You need a collection of pictures of people, all of whom are known to the learners, e.g. politicians, sportsmen, filmstars. (In the absence of pictures, written name slips may be used.) In addition, two sets of cards (pictures or written descriptions) are needed: (1) objects, actions or situations which may be given as rewards to those people of whom the learners approve, and (2) objects, actions or situations which may be given as punishments to those people of whom the learners disapprove. These 'reward' cards and 'punishment' cards should be used in the same way and with the same sort of language use as the 'present' cards in the main game, or in the same way as in Variation 1.

Sound games

Sound effects can create in the listener's mind an impression of people, places and actions. There is a demand for the listener to contribute through the imagination. This inevitably leads to individual interpretations, and individual interpretations lead to a need to exchange points of view and to express opinions and ideas.

This section of games, although concerned with listening, also gives rise to rich oral production.

40   Voices and objects

Language	Naming people and objects in response to a question, *Who am I?* or *What's this?*
Skills	Listening and speaking.
Control	Guided.
Level	Beginners.
Time	5–10 minutes.
Materials	A blindfold.

Preparation

None.

Procedure

Class work.

Blindfold a learner. Ask another learner to come forward and stand quietly next to the first and say something to him, for example, an English proverb, or a quotation from a song or rhyme, or textbook being studied by the class.

Learner 2: Who am I?
Learner 1: Michael?

Learner 2: No, listen.
　　　　　　To be or not to be, that is the question . . .
Learner 1: David!
Learner 2: Yes.
Learner 3: What's this? (*drops object on to desk*)
Learner 1: A key.
Learner 3: No, it isn't. (*drops object again*)
Learner 1: A coin.
Learner 3: Yes.

41　Actions by one person

Language	Narrating a sequence of events, using the present continuous (e.g. *He's opening some drawers*) and past simple (e.g. *He opened some drawers*).
Skills	Listening and speaking
Control	Guided.
Level	Beginners.
Time	10–15 minutes.
Materials	None.

Preparation

Write down a sequence of actions on a piece of paper (see *Procedure*).

Procedure

Class work.

So often the present continuous is practised in the classroom by reference to actions which are seen. In this game the learners close their eyes, listen and try to interpret what they hear.

Ask everyone to close their eyes and put their heads on their arms to reduce the chance of them sneaking a look!

Give a written sequence of actions to one learner to perform, e.g.

Walk quietly across the room to the teacher's desk.
Open and close all the drawers quietly.
Walk quietly to the cupboard.

Open the doors and then close them.
Walk quietly across the room.
Open the classroom door. Go out and close the door.

Ask the learner to do the sequence of actions twice. During the first sequence the class listen and say nothing. During the second sequence you can ask questions, e.g.

Teacher: What is he doing?
Class: He's walking.
Teacher: Is he walking quietly?
Class: Yes.
Teacher: Now, what is he doing?
Class: He's opening some drawers.

For the past simple, ask the class to describe the sequence of actions once they have been performed. If there are mistakes, perform the sequence again. Finally let everyone *see* the actions and confirm each description by using the present continuous.

42   Listening to sounds

Language	Naming and describing sounds, using the pattern *I can hear* . . . and the present continuous; also uncertainty indicated by *I think I can hear* . . . or *probably*.
Skills	Listening and speaking.
Control	Guided.
Level	Beginners/intermediate.
Time	5–10 minutes.
Materials	None.

Preparation

None.

Procedure

Class work.
   Ask everyone to close their eyes, perhaps even to rest their heads on

their arms. Ask the learners to listen carefully to every sound they can hear and to try to identify the sounds. They will be listening for all the 'natural' noises of the classroom, the building, and outside.

You might ask everyone to listen for two or three minutes and then to write down what they heard, or you could ask some learners to describe the noises as they hear them, e.g.

Learner 1: I can hear some girls.
            I can hear some girls playing.
            They are laughing and calling to each other. I think they are playing with a ball. Yes, I can hear it (bouncing).
Learner 2: I think I can hear a plane. It's probably coming into the airport.

43   Actions by two people or more

Language	Narrating a sequence of actions, using the past continuous (e.g. *Someone was hammering*), the past simple (e.g. *Someone came in*) and the present perfect (e.g. *He's (just) come into the room*).
Skills	Listening and speaking.
Control	Guided.
Level	Intermediate.
Time	10–15 minutes.
Materials	A hammer and a piece of wood.

Preparation

Write down two copies of a sequence of actions to be performed by two people (see *Procedure*).

Procedure

Class work.

Ask everyone to close their eyes and put their heads on their arms. Select two learners, and give them each a copy of the sequence of actions so that they know what to do, e.g.

A: At teacher's desk: hammers a nail into wood.

94

B: Opens door of room and says, 'Hi!'
A: Continues to hammer and says 'Hi!' followed immediately by 'Ouch!'
A: Drops hammer.
B: Quickly walks to A and pulls chair across for A to sit on.
A: Groans. Sits on chair, groans again.

Before the class open their eyes, A and B should return to their places.
Teacher: What happened?
Learner 1: Someone was hammering.
Learner 2: Then someone came in.
Learner 2: Then someone said, 'Ouch!'
Teacher: Why did he say, 'Ouch!'?
Learner 3: Because he hit himself with the hammer.
Teacher: Why did the person hit himself?
Learner 4: Probably because he looked up when he said, 'Hi!'

If there is some confusion over the sequence of events tell the class to close their eyes again and ask two learners to perform again. If the sequence was correctly reported ask everyone to watch the sequence again. Comment on it as it happens and then ask for a summary, e.g.

John was hammering on the desk when Helen came into the room. Helen said 'Hi!' and John looked up. When he looked up he hit his finger. Helen came across the room and got a chair. John sat down and groaned.

If this is followed by some similar sequence the language points will be well practised. The learners, in pairs or groups, could be asked to present their own sequences. (See also, 'Using the tape recorder', Game 44, example 3.)

44   Using the tape recorder

Language	Identifying and describing sounds, and narrating sequences of events, using various verb forms: present continuous (*The woman is singing*); present perfect (*He has opened the door*); past simple (*The dog barked*); future (*He's going to open a drawer*); expressing uncertainty (*I'm not sure . . . It could be . . .*)
Skills	Listening and speaking.
Control	Guided.
Level	Intermediate and advanced.
Time	20–30 minutes.
Materials	Tape recorder and tapes.

Preparation

Record, or ask your learners to record, the various sounds listed under *Procedure*.

Some excellent published material of this type is available: *Sounds Interesting*, by Alan Maley and Alan Duff, Cambridge University Press, 1975 (Teacher's Book and cassette); and *Sounds Intriguing*, by Alan Maley and Alan Duff, Cambridge University Press, 1979 (Teacher's Book and cassette).

Procedure

Class work or group work.

Below are three examples of the use of taped sounds.

Example 1
Door opening/closing – cigarette being lit – car being started and driven away – telephone ringing and being answered – watch and clock ticking – floor being brushed – cupboard being locked – dog barking – someone sneezing.

Questions include: (just before playing the sound) What is this?; (still playing) Is it a . . .?; (after playing) Was it a . . .? What was that? What was he doing? What was happening?

Example 2
For the present perfect we need an event (more than a minor action)
which has *just* been completed.
a) Washing up – pots put to dry – water poured away.
b) Alarm clock – groan of waking person – 'Oh dear!'
c) Typing-paper removed – signature made with pen.
d) Door opens – class comes in – they settle down.

Questions include: What has (just) happened?

Example 3 (sounds in sequence)
For the past simple a narrative episode is ideal. A sound story like the
one described below may also involve the use of various tense forms.

While the tape is playing: present continuous (*The woman is singing*)
and present simple (*She has some keys*); when you have stopped the
tape: present perfect (*He has opened the door*) and past
simple + while + past continuous (*The dog barked while she was
phoning the police*); when you play the tape again and stop it before the
action: future with going to (*He's going to open a drawer and take some
money*).

Radio music – radio switched off – door opened – bath water run –
singing of woman – splashes in bath (fades) – wind – car stops – door
opens and closes – footsteps up drive – rattle of keys – door opens –
little dog barks, then is kicked and howls – footsteps in hall (tiptoeing) –
door opened – drawer opened – money clinking – footsteps – dog snarls
– door opened – scream of woman – splash of bath water – running of
feet – opening and closing of door – splash of water – wet feet –
telephone being dialled (three numbers) – dog barks again – dog kicked
– howls again.

Warning: Material of this kind will be enjoyable and game-like as long
as the emphasis is placed on the mystery of sound and the fun of
interpreting it. Such material will become ordinary if the teacher tries to
'squeeze' too many language-teaching points out of it.

Story games

There are a number of reasons for the inclusion of this section: not least is the fact that so many examinations demand extensive writing. The games in this section, by their nature, provide a framework for learners to speak and write *at length* instead of engaging in short exchanges. Only interrupt a learner in order to help the story along. Should you decide that it might be helpful to correct certain errors that are made, then make a written or mental note of the errors during the story-telling, but delay dealing with them until afterwards.

45   Guess what I'm drawing

Language	Use of vocabulary items in reply to questions, perhaps in such sentence patterns as *I think it's going to be a . . .* or *It might be a . . .*
Skills	Listening and speaking.
Control	Guided.
Level	Beginners.
Time	5–10 minutes for class work. 10–15 minutes for pair work.
Materials	Chalkboard or OHP and paper and pencils for each learner.

Preparation

None.

Procedure

Class work, optionally leading to pair work.
    Start to draw on the board or OHP, asking, e.g.
Teacher: What am I drawing?
Class: A table.
Teacher: No. (*Continuing to draw*)
Class: A house?

Teacher: No, not exactly. (*Continuing to draw*)
Class: A shop.
Teacher: Yes, but what's happening?
Class: There's a tree . . .
Teacher: No.
Class: A fire. The shop is burning!
Teacher: Yes. Now who is this?
Class: The shopkeeper.
Teacher: And what's he doing?

The learners might then play this game in pairs.

46 Silly stories

Language	Making up stories, using the past tense.
Skills	Listening and speaking.
Control	Free.
Level	Intermediate/advanced.
Time	5–10 minutes.
Materials	None.

Preparation

None, unless you would like to think of some beginnings for stories (see *Procedure*).

Procedure

Class work.
   Begin the story with the first half of a sentence. Then ask the class to think of a continuation, e.g.
Teacher: I saw a horse sitting . . .
Learner 1: . . . in the kitchen.
Teacher: It was eating . . .
Learner 2: . . . a piece of cake.
Learner 3: And drinking a cup of tea.
Teacher: I said . . .
Learner 4: 'Don't you have milk in your tea?'

47 Fantasy stories

Language	Making up stories, using all the language at the learner's command, particularly past tense verb forms.
Skills	All.
Control	Free.
Level	Intermediate/advanced.
Time	30 minutes.
Materials	Magazine pictures; paper and pencils, or tape recorders (optional). In Variations 2 and 3, objects and pictures.

Preparation

Each pair or group will need 15–20 pictures cut from magazines. *Any* pictures will do, but they should show a variety of places and objects and include several people.

Procedure

Group or pair work, leading to class work.

The object of the game is to invent a complete fantasy based on the pictures received. It should *not* be realistic about someone losing their purse or having a party, for example. The pair or group should invent the story through discussion.

Once the story is ready, it should be written down and/or recorded on tape.

The stories should then be told to the whole class.

The pictures and the written version of the stories could be displayed on the wall.

Variation 1

Group or pair work, leading to class work.

Instead of giving each pair or group a selection of pictures, put 15–20 pictures on the wall of the classroom.

Then ask the pairs or groups to invent a story, making use of the pictures *in any order*.

When everyone has finished, the stories can be written down and told.

The advantage of this variation is that each group will be more interested in what the others have written, because the same pictures have been used.

Variation 2
Group work leading to class work.

Instead of using only pictures, prepare a kit containing six to ten assorted objects and pictures, e.g. a piece of string, a key, a toy car, a picture of an expensive house, a picture of a bank, a whistle, an empty purse or wallet.

Each group works independently to prepare a short play to 'reconstruct a crime', and must refer to all the objects and pictures. Each play is then presented to the class.

Variation 3
Group work.

Each learner in a group is given a picture or an object. The learners then take turns to tell a story. They must continue the story as told by their neighbour and must refer to the picture or object at some point in their continuation of the story.

Variation 4
Class work based on pair or individual work.

Discuss with the learners the kind of subjects which are reported on the radio news. List these subjects on the board. Now ask each learner (or pair of learners) to write out a *completely ludicrous* news report. If possible, ask each pair to read out their news.

Variation 5
Group work.

This variation is principally a matter of organisation. Give each group between four and six pictures. The group should study the pictures, discuss the content and interpret what they find. The group should then invent a story based on the pictures placed in a sequence.

Then all the groups should leave their pictures in sequence and move to another group's pictures. *Each group should leave one learner behind*. The new group should then look at the pictures and the sequence they are in. The new group should try to imagine what story was invented by the previous group. They may ask questions and seek confirmation from the learner left behind by the previous group.

Note: You can introduce further variety and increase the demands on the learners by asking them to tell their stories as if they are telling them to a certain type of listener, for example, a young child, an elderly person, a policeman, a friend, a teacher, a doctor, an employer, a customer: some of these will be appropriate, some may not.

48   Build a story

Language	Narrative and descriptive language in a past or a present tense. Giving instructions (imperatives), e.g. *Draw . . . , Put . . . .* Linking devices, e.g. *and then . . . , after that . . . , next . . . , finally . . . .*
Skills	Listening and speaking.
Control	Guided.
Level	Intermediate/advanced.
Time	20 minutes.
Materials	Chalkboard or OHP.

Preparation

It would be a good idea for you to try sketching out a picture and imagining some possible ways the story might develop.

Procedure

Class work.

This activity does rather depend on your (or one of your student's) ability to draw quickly. The drawing does *not* need to be good!

Essentially, you begin to draw a large picture on the board or OHP. From the moment you begin, invite description and interpretation of what you are doing. If you remain *totally* silent the effect, though somewhat bizarre to begin with, can be impressive. The learners feel responsible for the story. You can mix your role: you can confirm a suggested interpretation as if the story already exists in your mind or you can accept another interpretation which will lead the story away from the one you had planned. Also, sometimes you can add a piece to the drawing and then ask the learners to interpret it; on other occasions you can ask (through gesture only!) what you should add next.

When you and the class feel the story is complete you can speak!

Congratulate them. Then ask each student to reconstruct the story and
to prepare to tell it to their neighbour. This will demonstrate that each
person experienced the story differently.

Example
Little girl goes to wood / mother worried / black clouds come / mother
desperate, goes into dark wood / dragon comes along and burns house
to the ground / mother finds little girl in lovely house in dark wood and
they live there happily ever after.

49   Confabulation, or the key sentence

Language	Making up a story or play around a given sentence.
Skills	All.
Control	Free.
Level	Advanced
Time	30–40 minutes.
Materials	None.

Preparation

You may like to prepare a list of unlikely sentences (see *Procedure*).

Procedure

Group or pair work, leading to class work.

Each group or pair is given an unlikely sentence which is kept a secret from the others, e.g.

I always eat trout for breakfast.
I opened the door and saw an elephant.
So I replied, 'Never on a Sunday'.

Each group prepares a story or a play which includes the sentence exactly as it has been given, as naturally as possible. The group tells the story or acts out the play for the others, who have to try to spot the given sentence.

50 Consequences

Language	Making up sentences, using the past tense according to a given pattern; asking questions and giving answers about the sentences.
Skills	All.
Control	Guided.
Level	Intermediate.
Time	10 minutes.
Materials	A piece of paper for each learner.

Preparation

None.

Procedure

Group work leading to class work.

Demonstrate the idea. Fold a piece of paper in half, then into quarters and eighths; all the folds should be parallel. Then, guided by these folds, refold the paper into a concertina. As each person writes, he/she should only look at his/her fold.

Learner 1: . . . (a man's name) met
Learner 2: . . . (a woman's name) at/in
Learner 3: . . . (a place)
Learner 4: He said . . .
Learner 5: She said . . .
Learner 6: And so they . . .

```
Winston Churchill
met
Doris Day
in
the Tower of London
He said, Do you like dancing?
She said, You're too fat.
And so they drank tea.
```

When the last person has written on the last fold ask him/her to read it all out.

Other versions in this 'story' might be as follows:

Learner 1:	If . . .	If . . .
	met	had met
Learner 2:	. . .	. . .
	in	at
Learner 3:	. . .	. . .
Learner 4:	He would say . . .	He would have said . . .
Learner 5:	She would answer . . .	She would have answered . . .
Learner 6:	And so they would . . .	And so they would have . . .

There could be some discussion of the results, but discussion should be in the spirit of the game and not become mere mechanical transformation of tenses, e.g.

Who met A? Who did B meet? Where did they meet? What did he/she say? What happened? What would he/she really have said? What would you say if you met A in a bookshop?

Variation
Group work leading to class work.

In many countries it is customary, on New Year's Day, to promise improved behaviour for the following year. The idea of the 'New Year's Resolution' provides a basis for a variation of the 'Consequences' game.

Each group or row of players has a sheet of paper. The first player writes: *I, (name), promise to . . .*

Then he/she folds the paper so that what he/she has written is hidden and passes the paper to the next player. This player writes a New Year's Resolution, e.g. *stop smoking/work harder*, etc.

He/she folds the paper again and passes it on. The third player writes: *provided that* (name) *promises to . . .*

He/she again folds the paper and passes it on to a fourth player who writes a second New Year's Resolution.

The whole message is passed to a fifth player who reads it out to the class.

51   Bits and pieces

Language	Narrating and describing, principally in the present tense. Speculating, using e.g. *Perhaps . . . , might be . . . , could be . . . , I think . . . .* Asking questions.
Skills	Listening, speaking and writing.
Control	Guided/free.
Level	All.
Time	15–40 minutes.
Materials	Picture-strip stories, or texts.

Preparation

You need one picture-strip story for one group in the basic game. In Variation 1 you can use one picture-strip story for a class. In Variations 2, 3, 4 and 5 you need a text at an appropriate level for your learners. In Variation 6 you need two texts. Cut the strip into separate pictures or cut your text into separate sentences, paragraphs or single words.

Procedure

Group work.

Give each learner in a group one picture from the strip. If there are extra pictures you may either give them to the more able learners or not give them to anyone, thus deliberately creating a gap. Each learner must describe his/her picture but not show it to the others; the others may ask questions about it. The aim of the group is to try to establish what the story might be. They should write down their idea of the story and then put the pictures together in what they believe is the correct order. You can then check what they have done and tell them how near they managed to get.

Variation 1
Class work based on groups.

The groups should be small; about three or four learners. Give each group one picture from a strip story. They should then study it and decide what is happening in it.

Then say that each group may send two learners to two other groups to find out what *their* pictures are about. This information must be conveyed orally and not visually, i.e. not by looking at the picture.

After collecting information about the other pictures, each group should then try to imagine what the complete story must be. At this point you can ask each group to relate their story. However, you can continue with group work in the following way. Make up *new* groups comprising one learner from each of the previous groups. The various ideas for the completed story can then be related and discussed.

Variation 2
Group work.

Texts cut into separate sentences or paragraphs may be used. Each learner should receive one sentence (or several if you prefer – and they need not be sentences from the same part of the text). Each learner should read their sentence. And then the group should try to agree on the order of them in order to make up the complete story.

Variation 3
Class work.

Each learner should receive one sentence. He/she should memorise the sentence, then give the paper back to you. The learners then walk about in the classroom telling other learners what their sentence is and listening to the others. *Their aim is to establish what the story is.* They then arrange themselves in a line in the order of the sentences they believe relate the story. And then they each, in turn, say their sentence.

Variation 4
Group work.

Each learner is given one (or several) paragraphs. These are studied and not shown to the others. The learners then tell the group the content of their texts. (They do not *read* the text.) After listening to everyone, the group discusses the sequence of each text and determines the story. When everyone in the group feels sure the story is correct the texts can be placed together in order and the story read out.

Variation 5
Group work.

Each learner is given a word on a piece of card. The words in the appropriate order make up a sentence. The aim of the students is to find what the sentence is and to put the cards in order – possibly even standing in order and showing their card.

Variation 6

Group work or class work.

In this variation you must provide the texts of two different stories cut up into individual sentences (or sequences of sentences). Each learner is given one sentence. The learners must compare their own sentence with the sentences of other learners. They should join the learners they believe have related sentences from the same story as their own, and try to work out what the complete text is.

Clearly, for a class you will need longer texts than for a group. It is easier to do in a group than in a class.

Note: The same game can be done by a pair or an individual sorting out the muddled sentences on a desk.

52 Domino story

Language	Narrative.
Skills	Listening and speaking.
Control	Free.
Level	All.
Time	At least 20 minutes.
Materials	Picture dominoes (see *Preparation*).

Preparation

You or your learners must make the dominoes. (See illustration.) The easiest and fastest method is to use simple drawings. It is not necessary for you to try to produce pictures which link together in one clear story. However, it does help if the characters remain the same.

Procedure

Group work.

Each learner is given five dominoes with a picture rather than a number at each end. The learner may lay a domino down next to another domino if he/she can continue the story by referring to the picture which he/she is building on to.

The ingenuity lies in arguing the connection, e.g.

He was miserable and frightened. So he ran out of the wood as fast as possible. When he got home he had a cup of hot soup, etc.

53   Change the story

Language	Narrative, with emphasis on verbs.
Skills	All the skills, based on writing.
Control	Free.
Level	Intermediate/advanced.
Time	30–40 minutes.
Materials	Paper and pencils/pens.

Preparation

None.

Procedure

Group work.

Each learner writes a short story or description. He/she must underline all the verbs in the story. The group then compiles a list of about twenty verbs at random. Then each learner reads out his/her story omitting the verbs. As he/she pauses in place of a verb the other learners in the group supply a verb at random from the list. Alternatively, each learner substitutes a verb at random into the text before reading it. The result can be very amusing.

54 Leonardo's strip!

Language	Narrative.
Skills	All the skills, principally writing.
Control	Free.
Level	All.
Time	30 minutes.
Materials	'Doodle strips' (see *Preparation*).

Preparation

Either you or the students must prepare the doodle strips. Doodle strips are made of four or five little pictures which may be completely abstract or may illustrate recognisable things. The learners must not feel that they have to find *your* story line. It is better for you not to have one! The pictures must be an ambiguous starting point for *their* imaginations.

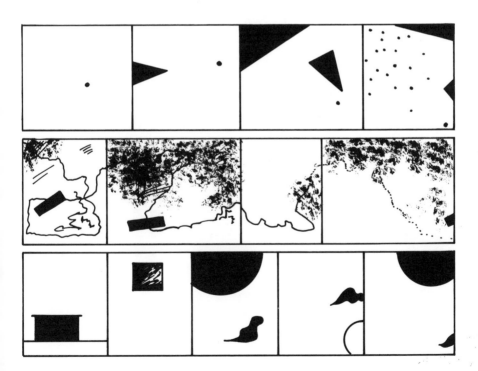

Procedure

Pair or individual work.

Essentially the learners are writing stories based on the pictures. You might ask one or two learners to read their stories out. Much greater exploitation may be gained by using the organisation proposed in Game 47, *Fantasy Stories*, Variation 5.

Acknowledgement: We would like to acknowledge Leonardo da Vinci for suggesting that we look at peeling walls to see landscapes and battles; and John Morgan and Mario Rinvolucri, who present the idea of doodle strips in their book, *Once Upon a Time* (Cambridge University Press 1983). They in turn acknowledge Mo Strangeman.

Word games

In this section the focus of attention is initially on the word rather than the sentence: spelling (as, for example, in *Dash it and hang it*), meanings (as in *Definitions* or *The odd man out*), words for sentence-making (as in *A–A, B–B* or *Make a sentence*), words as inferred from contexts (as in *Missing words*), or words as categorised according to grammatical usage (as in Variation 3 of *Bingo*). However, learners are required in many cases to go beyond the initial focus and to communicate in full sentences, sometimes (as in the variation of *The odd man out*) to pursue ideas and argue at some length.

All levels of proficiency are catered for by one or more of the games in this section.

55   Bingo

Language	Listening to and reading numbers, or, in Variation 1, words, or, in Variation 2, whole sentences. The words and sentences can be selected to practise any area of language that you wish. Variation 3 practises identification of parts of speech.
Skills	All.
Control	Controlled.
Level	Beginners, except for Variations 2 and 3, which are suitable for intermediate learners also.
Time	10–20 minutes.
Materials	Paper and pencil for yourself and each learner.

Preparation

Decide on a group of numbers you wish to practise, totalling not more than about 25. These may be sequences (e.g. 1–25) or a selection of

numbers which present listening problems (e.g. 13 and 30, 19 and 90).
Either write them on the board or tell the learners what they are.

Procedure

Class work.
   Tell the learners to write down any four of the numbers from those
you have given them. Call the numbers in random order. The learners
must cross out the numbers they have written if they hear them called.
The first learner to cross out all four of his/her numbers calls out 'Bingo'
and reads out the four numbers to prove the claim.
   It is possible to play the game selecting more than four numbers from
a group larger than 25. However, this will take more time.

Warning: Make a note of each number as you call it out. This will help
you to avoid calling out the numbers more than once.

Variation 1
Class work.
   Instead of listing out 25 numbers, as above, choose a group of words
you would like the learners to revise, for example, concerning clothing,
office equipment, food, etc.
   Write these on the board and follow the procedure described above.
   Instead of calling out four of the words you may choose to give four
definitions of words on the board. This makes the game more of a
challenge.

Variation 2
Class work.
   Write, or ask the learners to write, about ten short sentences on the
board. These might all include prepositions, e.g.

The chemist's shop is on the right of the bank.
The chemist's shop is in front of the bank.
The bank is on the right of the post office, behind the library.
The grocer's shop is behind the library.
The toilets are in the park.
The toilets are in front of the park.
The road goes over the bridge.
The road goes under the bridge.

The sentences may also concern actions, perhaps taken from a picture
or pictures, e.g.

The man is drinking tea.

The electrician is repairing the plug.
The woman is typing.

The learners choose any four sentences and illustrate them with quick sketches. The game is then played as above.

By using pictures, the learners' attention is focussed on the meaning of the sentences, whereas in Variation 1 the learners merely associate the sound of a word with its written form.

Variation 3
Class work.

If you should want the learners to practise categorising words according to parts of speech, you could adapt *Bingo* for that purpose as follows. Provide each learner with a card or piece of paper marked off with six squares (or 'boxes'), one for each part of speech.

Each learner decides which part of speech he/she is going to listen out for and writes them into the top of each of their boxes. They might choose from: verb, article, noun, adverb, adjective, pronoun, preposition, conjunction etc. Such distinctions as 'verb of motion', 'verb – past tense', 'plural noun', 'singular noun', etc. may of course be added with your guidance. You can in this way give practice in the recognition and identification of *any* parts of speech.

A learner might decide to have more than one box for a part of speech. As you call out words from a prepared miscellaneous list, the learners write them into the correct square on their grid. They only need one word in each box in order to say, *Bingo!*

56   Dash it and hang it

Language	Guessing, inferring, suggesting. In the basic game and Variation 1, the focus is on combining letters to spell a mystery word. In Variation 2, the focus is on combining words to make a sentence.
Skills	All.
Control	Guided.
Level	Beginners/intermediate.
Time	2–3 minutes.
Materials	Chalkboard or OHP; in the variations, if played in pairs, paper and pencils; in Variation 2, a picture (optional).

Preparation

None.

Procedure

Class work.

Think of a five-letter word, for example, and draw the same number of dashes on the board. The learners call out words of five letters. If any of these words contain a letter which is in the word you are thinking of *and* is in the same position, write the letter on the board, over the appropriate dash. For example, you are thinking of MOUTH, and a learner calls out TEACH. The letter H is in both words, and is in the same position, so you write:

$$\_ \ \_ \ \_ \ \_ \ \overset{H}{\_}$$

Suppose, however, that the learner had called out RADIO. Although the letter O is in both RADIO and MOUTH, it is *not* in the same position, so you would not write anything.

A more complicated and demanding way of playing this game is as follows. When a learner calls out a word with a letter (or letters) in the same position as in your mystery word, write their word below the dashes on the board, and merely say, 'One letter' (or whatever the number), but do not say which letter (or letters) it is. Eventually, the learners should have a list of words from which they can make a guess as to the identity of some of the key letters. For example:

```
_  _  _  _  _
R  A  D  I  O     (no letters)
T  E  A  C  H     (one letter)
T  E  E  T  H     (two letters)
W  A  T  C  H     (one letter)
B  E  L  O  W     (no letters)
M  O  N  T  H     (four letters)
```

At this point, the learners may well agree that they can ask for T and H to be written above the dashes.

Variation 1
Class work or pair work.

A version of the above game is the well-known *Hangman*, which may be played with the whole class or in pairs.

Draw one dash for each letter of the word you are thinking of. The other player(s) suggest a letter which they think may be in the word. If it

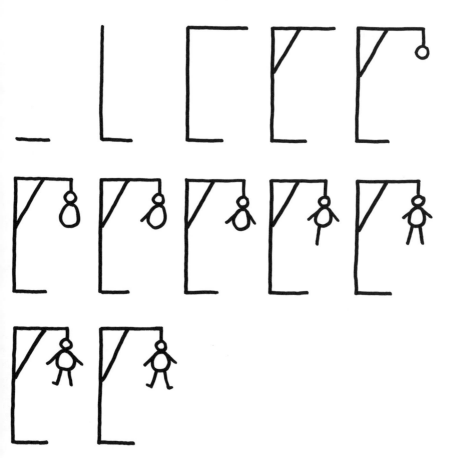

is, write it in above the appropriate dash. If it is not, draw one part of the 'hanged man' as in the illustration. Thirteen mistakes 'hangs' the other player(s).

(Thirteen is thought to be an unlucky number. In pre-Hellenic times the king, who only ruled for a year, was sacrificed in the thirteenth month. There was a thirteen-month year at that time.)

Variation 2
Class work or pair work.

A variation of *Hangman* may be played in which each dash represents a *word*, instead of a letter as above. When all the words have been correctly guessed and filled in, the result is a meaningful sentence. It helps if the topic of the sentence is stated before the game starts, or is contextualised by a picture.

57 A–A, B–B

Language	Revision of vocabulary items according to categories, e.g. colour; making of sentences containing selected vocabulary items; remembering and repeating.
Skills	Listening, speaking and writing.
Control	Guided.
Level	Beginners/intermediate.
Time	15 minutes.
Materials	Paper and pencils; dictionaries, textbooks (optional).

Preparation

Select several sentence patterns suitable for using with vocabulary items that are to be revised.

Procedure

Group work leading to team contest.

Give the learners time to work in groups to compile lists of words, all beginning with a given letter, organised according to one or more categories. (Dictionaries and textbooks may be consulted.) For example, the following lists of colours and common objects beginning with the letter B might be compiled:

Colours	Objects
beige	bag
black	ball
blue	bed
brown	bell
buff	boat
	book
	box

Other categories which might be suitable for this game include: articles of clothing, shops, vehicles, animals, occupations, verbs of motion, adjectives of size.

When the learners are ready, divide them into teams and give the opening of your selected sentence to a representative of one team, e.g.
Teacher: I went shopping and I bought . . .

The team representative must repeat what you have said, and complete the sentence using a word (or words) from the given category (or categories), remembering as best as he/she can the preparatory work just done in groups, plus any other ideas that may spring to mind, e.g.

Learner: I went shopping and I bought a blue bag, a black box, a brown . . .

Repetition of any key word within a sentence is against the rules of the game, and so are hesitations of more than a few seconds. For either fault, the individual must stop, and another representative, from the opposing team, must then be given another (similar) sentence to complete, e.g.

Teacher: In the shopping precinct I saw . . .

Again, self-repetition by the representative is against the rules, but repetition of what other players have said earlier, in the context of other sentences, *is* allowed, indeed is to be encouraged, since in that way it will enable players to learn from listening to each other.

The object of the game is to see how long and elaborate a sentence the teams' representatives can devise. The longest sentence, containing no self-repetitions, and spoken without undue hesitation, wins.

Variation

Group work or class work.

The players should, preferably, be in a circle, but this is not essential.

In this game, a given sentence pattern must be completed by adding any words that make sense, one word being added by a player on any one occasion. Each player must repeat verbatim whatever has been said by the previous player before adding a word of his/her own. So, for example, if the given sentence pattern is 'I went shopping and I bought . . .', the fifth player might say:

Learner: I went shopping and I bought a shirt, a skirt, a sausage, an apple and a *car*.

There is no need to restrict the added words to those beginning with a particular letter of the alphabet, unless you wish to make the game trickier, for variety's sake. Of course, many sentence patterns may be used in the game, besides the example given here. The best known, to children and language teachers alike, is the classic 'The minister's cat is . . .'

58   Make a sentence

Language	Making (and re-making) sentences; requesting, suggesting, discussing choice of words for sentences.
Skills	All.
Control	Guided.
Level	Beginners/intermediate.
Time	At least 35 minutes.
Materials	Strips of paper; in the variation, chalkboard and die (optional).

Preparation

Cut strips of paper to a standard size (about 10 cm × 3 cm), sufficient for each learner to write sentences, one word per strip.

In the variation, you will need strips of different colours (see below), one colour for each type of word in whatever sentence pattern you decide to use for the game.

Procedure

Individual work leading to class/group work.

Each learner writes out a sentence of his/her own making – legibly! *Each word of the sentence should be on a separate strip of paper.*

All the learners' strips of paper should be put in a box and mixed together. Then each learner takes out the same number of strips as he/she put in, not looking at them, but taking them out randomly.

The aim of the game is for all the players to cooperate in making as many new sentences as possible by recombining their words. They should move freely about the class, looking at each other's words and working in twos and threes wherever they see an opportunity to make a sentence, or sentences.

Whenever a group succeeds in making a sentence from the words in their possession, they should show it to you. If you accept it as a well-formed sentence, lay it on a desk or table where everyone can see it.

When a player has got rid of all his/her word strips, he/she must help others who are still trying to make sentences from theirs. If possible, *all* players' word strips must be used in sentences. Sentences already laid down may be altered, or added to; they may even be broken up for recombining with other words to make new sentences, provided that no word is left over at the end.

Variation
Class work leading to group work.
This variation is a more controlled version of the game described above.
Collect words from the learners in a class discussion according to stated grammatical categories (e.g. articles, adjectives, nouns, verbs), and write them on the board in columns, as in a substitution table. The table may be very controlled so that only grammatically correct sentences will result when single words from each of the columns are combined, e.g.

I	2	3	4	5
A	boy	bought	a	model plane.
The	girl	sold	my	book.
	soldier	broke		cabbage.
	grocer	etc.		gun.
	teacher			
				etc.
	etc.			

More ambitiously, substitution tables may be constructed that might result in grammatically *in*correct sentences, as well as absurd ones, unless the learners are careful in how they combine words from the columns, e.g.

I	2	3	4
The	typewriter	is	broken.
A	brother	are	lost.
My	friends	was	happy.
My father's	book	were	expensive.
Their	books		
			etc.
etc.	etc.		

With help from the learners, copy the collection of words from the board on to strips of card. Colour code these according to grammatical categories i.e. put all the words from any one column on strips of card of the same colour. Thus, verbs might be red, nouns blue, adjectives green, etc. Your colour coding should, of course, reflect the level of understanding of your learners. Some (but not all) may benefit from having the subjects of sentences distinguished from the objects. Only you can judge what is appropriate, and useful.

Shuffle each category of word cards in turn, i.e. keep the different colours separate. Give one card from each category to each and every group of learners in the class. (Groups should consist of three or four, or more.) When all the groups have a complete set of cards, i.e. one of each colour (one from each column of the substitution table) they must try and arrange them so that they make a sentence that is grammatically well formed *and* makes sense. If this proves impossible – as indeed it probably will, provided that a sufficient variety of word cards of each category have been collected and shuffled – then groups should exchange word cards until as many acceptable sentences as possible have been made.

Note: An alternative method of distributing word cards randomly among the groups is to give each group a die, which they throw a stipulated number of times, depending on how many cards you intend them to receive. A group representative should note the numbers thrown, e.g. 1, 1, 4, 6, 2, 6. Each number, from 1 to 6, should be linked to a different category of word, e.g. 1 – article, 2 – adjective, 3 – noun, 4– verb, 5 – adverb, 6 – conjunction. Each group receives one card of the appropriate category for each number that was thrown. (It may be that a second throw of the die and distribution of word cards will be required half way through a game, should too few words of a particular category be in circulation.)

59 The odd man out

Language	Giving reasons, using *because*; answering questions, agreeing and disagreeing. The game is ideal for revising lexical sets, e.g. words for colours, family relations, animals, household utensils.
Skills	All.
Control	Guided.
Level	Intermediate; advanced in the variation.
Time	10 minutes.
Materials	Chalkboard, OHP, or paper.

Preparation

Prepare 10–15 groups of words, each of which contains an 'odd man out', e.g.
a) horse, cow, mouse, *knife*, fish
b) David, Michael, Andrew, *Alison*, Adrian
c) *plate*, bean, soup, sandwich, apple
d) *bicycle*, bus, car, motorcycle, lorry
e) green, *big*, orange, brown, red
f) brother, father, *sister*, uncle, grandfather
g) June, January, March, *Spring*, May
h) Austin, *Volvo*, Morris, Jaguar
i) Shakespeare, Milton, J. B. Priestley, *Laurence Olivier*
j) Paris, Ottawa, *New York*, London

The words used should, of course, reflect the interests of the learners and could be of a specialist nature.

They can be presented on a chalkboard, an OHP, or on sheets of paper.

Procedure

Class work.

The learners write down the word from the first group which they think is the 'odd man out'. Individuals are then asked to say which is the 'odd man out' and to say why.

The other players should be asked if they agree; if they disagree, to say why. The teacher should not say which answer he/she thinks is correct until this discussion is finished – partly because this would inhibit discussion and partly because there may be no *one* correct answer, and the learners should be encouraged to find as many possible answers as they can. Each of the groups of words can be discussed in turn in this way.

If any learner experiences difficulty here, the teacher can help by asking leading questions, for example, for (j) above:
Teacher: What is the capital of France/Canada/the USA/England?

Variation
Group or pair work.

This game is for advanced learners and mainly for use in group work or pair work.

Words should be selected which have no *obvious* connection, e.g. knife, saucepan, box, ruler, cabbage, bottle, typewriter, hammer, book.

The words could be photocopied for each group or could be on the board or OHP.

The aim of the game is to find different ways of classifying *four* of the words in each group. It is essential that the player can argue the case for his proposed classification, however eccentric it may be.

Common ways of classifying may refer to the material the objects are made of, their usage, their size, cost or shape. Less common classifications might be origin (for example, cabbage is not found in West Africa but the other objects are); or naturalness (cabbage is grown and not manufactured like the others); or more unexpected classifications (for example, typewriter has ten letters and all the others have eight letters or less).

You can give advanced learners the experience of classifying things from standpoints that are different from their own. Ask them, for example, to classify luxurious cars, street violence, tax avoidance, meditation, hard work, free legal aid, pop music, etc. first according, for example, to a pacifist's value system, then from the sort of point of view that we might expect to find in an advertising executive. The resulting classifications, including the 'odd man out', should of course be explained and justified in discussion.

Warning: The game will work only if the learners have sufficient command of the language to be able to name such categories as *size*, *quantity*, *quality*, *speed* and *texture* – that is to say, the categories which unite the companion words in each game. You may have to teach the learners the words for these categories, concentrating on a few each time you play 'The odd man out', and directing the learners to confine themselves to these when they devise their own examples.

60 Connections

Language	Asking for and giving reasons, using *Why . . .? Because . . .*
Skills	Listening and speaking, and in Variation 4, reading.
Control	Guided.
Level	Intermediate/advanced.
Time	5–10 minutes.
Materials	None, except in the variations, where pictures are required and, in Variation 4, a dictionary for each learner.

Preparation

None.

Procedure

Class, group or pair work.

Each learner in turn says a word he associates with the word given by the learner before him. This should be done as a fast game. Sometimes you or another learner may interrupt and ask why a word was chosen, e.g.

Learner 1: Water.
Learner 2: Tap.
Learner 3: Shoulder.
Teacher: Why did you say shoulder?
Learner 3: Because I thought of the sentence, 'A tap on the shoulder!'
Learner 4: Coat.
Learner 5: Joseph.
Teacher: Why did you say Joseph?
Learner 5: Because Joseph had a famous coat.
Learner 6: Egypt.

Variation 1
Class or group work.

Take two pictures at random and ask the learners to suggest a connection between them. It is better if the pictures show only a single object, person or place. Some learners will suggest very reasonable connections. Some learners will suggest crazy connections. In one sense, the latter are more 'meaningful' since more people will pay attention and think about them! This game may be played in groups, as well as with the whole class.

Variation 2
Class or group work.

Instead of taking pictures at random, as in Variation 1, you might make a consistent choice, for example, people and places. Thus:
Learner: She's going to the bank to get some money.
   or: He's the headteacher of that school.
   or: She's going to complain. They have sold her some bad fruit in that shop.

Variation 3
Group work.

A more challenging version of the game requires the learners to place a limited number of pictures – perhaps nine or twelve – on to the squares of a grid that has been drawn on a sheet of card or paper. The squares should, of course, be of a size to accommodate the pictures neatly. The pictures should be mounted on squares of card which are all the same size. The object of the game is to arrange the pictures on the grid in such a way that there are similarities between all the pictures in all the rows and columns, i.e. the lines of pictures that extend from top to bottom of the grid should all have some common feature, however small, that can be explained and justified, and so should the lines of pictures that extend from side to side. Discussion concerning how to arrange the pictures should be a cooperative, not a competitive, activity. The game is judged to be finished only when all the players agree, or agree to differ.

Variation 4
Class work.

This variation may be called a 'dictionary dash'. It gives practice in the reading skills of skimming and scanning a text at speed. Each learner needs his/her own copy of a dictionary. The learners are given a word, and, starting together, they must search through their dictionaries for another word containing the same number of letters. They must be able to argue a connection between the meaning of that word and the starting word.

61 Missing words

Language	Reading out loud, comparing, checking, discussing.
Skills	All.
Control	Guided.
Level	Intermediate/advanced.
Time	Depends on the length of the text chosen for the game.
Materials	Photocopies of texts at an appropriate level.

Preparation

Take two photocopies of the same text. White out different words in each text; or, if you want to give the learners additional problems, white out the *same* words in some cases, but not in all. Photocopy each of the resulting (i.e. whited out) texts in equal numbers, sufficient for a copy of the two different texts to be given to each pair of learners in the class.

Procedure

Pair work.

Each learner has one text and does not let his/her partner see it. Through reading and discussion they compile a complete text and write it down.

62 Additions

Language	Making phrases and sentences in cooperation with others; discussion.
Skills	Listening, speaking and writing.
Control	Guided.
Level	Intermediate/advanced.
Time	5 minutes or more.
Materials	Paper and pencils.

Preparation

None.

Procedure

Group work leading to class work.

The first player in each group says a word. (You may wish to stipulate what this first word is, so that all groups start off the same.) The second player decides on a word that will make some sort of sense when put either in front of the first word or after it. He/she says the two words together for the other players in the group to hear. The third player decides on a word that will make sense when put in front of or after the second player's two words. He/she says the resulting phrase of three words . . . and so on, round and round the group. The object is to make as long a sentence as possible by adding words one by one in this way.

One person in each group must write down the words as they accumulate. Finally, in a class discussion, ask all the group secretaries to read out their completed sentences for the others to judge if they are grammatically well formed and make sense, e.g.

Learner 1: Cat.
Learner 2: Black cat.
Learner 3: Black cat climbs.
Learner 4: The black cat climbs.
Learner 5: The black cat climbs high . . .
etc.

63   Definitions

Language	Asking for and giving definitions of words. The question word *What . . .?* is used, also *How . . .? Where . . .?* etc.
Skills	Listening and speaking.
Control	Guided.
Level	Advanced.
Time	10–15 minutes.
Materials	None.

Preparation

Choose a few words for the learners to define. Here are some examples: wall, typewriter, window, drum, garage, pen, ice-cream, cup of tea, penny, slice of bread.

Procedure

Class work leading to pair work.

Giving definitions of words may appear to be a traditional language learning activity! However, the approach below transforms this rather dull business into an exciting challenge! The idea is continually to challenge the player to define nearly every word he/she uses, in order to define the word you originally gave. Other learners should, of course, be asked to join in, by asking them to define words, e.g.

Teacher: What does 'wall' mean?

Learner 1: A wall is a vertical division, often made out of stone, bricks or concrete.

Learner 2: What is concrete?

Learner 1: Concrete is a material made out of sand, cement and small stones.

Learner 3: What is cement?

Learner 1: Cement is made out of limestone.

(Most questions will begin with *What* . . .? However, you may ask *How* . . .? and *Where* . . .? etc.)

Learner 4: How is limestone made into cement?

Learner 1: Er . . . I don't know!

You should limit each game by allowing no more than six requests for definitions or by an admission of inability to define a word.

Warning: Too strict a control over the grammatical form of the definitions will curtail goodwill and willingness to 'have a go'. Encourage a light-hearted, inventive and occasionally fanciful attitude!

64 Daft definitions

Language	Making, comparing and discussing definitions of words; making sentences; consulting the dictionary.
Skills	All.
Control	Guided.
Level	Advanced.
Time	10–20 minutes.
Materials	Dictionaries; written definitions of words; paper and pencils.

Preparation

Choose unfamiliar words from the dictionary which the learners use; write a definition and exemplifying sentence for each.

Procedure

Individual/group work leading to class discussion.

In the simplest version of this game, you choose an unfamiliar word from the learners' dictionary, copy out the definition given (or write one yourself), and then write a sentence exemplifying its meaning and use. Then write two or three false, but plausible, definitions for the same word, again with exemplifying sentences, also false. Read all your definitions and sentences to the class, for the learners to decide which one is correct and which ones are false. You may want to organise the class into groups, each of which must be supplied with a written copy of your definitions and sentences, to allow for preliminary discussion before a full class discussion. Once a decision has been reached, or the learners agree to differ, tell them to consult their dictionaries and check for themselves.

Once the class is accustomed to the game, ask individual learners to prepare definitions of words and exemplifying sentences for the rest of the class. This could well be done for homework. Alternatively, ask groups of learners to do this preparation cooperatively. An added complexity, which should add to the fun, is to permit the mixing-in of an *imaginary* word, complete with definition and sentence, along with a number of genuine words.

65 Deletions

Language	Discussion of meanings and changes of meanings; reading out loud; making suggestions; agreeing and disagreeing.
Skills	Listening, speaking and reading.
Control	Guided.
Level	Advanced.
Time	At least 10–15 minutes.
Materials	Chalkboard or strips of card.

Preparation

You should select a suitable complex sentence; you can copy the sentence on to strips of card, one per word (optional).

Procedure

Class work.

Write a complex sentence on the board, or on strips of card (one word per strip), which you should then affix to a wall or display board. (Although preparing strips of card takes time, it is preferable to the board since the game can be played more easily this way.)

Tell the learners that the object of the game is to take the given sentence and reduce it, step by step, to the shortest possible length, compatible with grammatical correctness and sense.

At each step, a deletion must be made that entails (a) the removal of one word, or (b) the removal of two consecutive words, or (c) the removal of three consecutive words. (Two or three words that are separated in the sentence by other words may *not* be deleted.) The punctuation of the sentence may be altered at any time as required, and the meaning of the increasingly short sentences that result from the deletions may also be altered: i.e. may be different from the meaning of preceding sentences. (It would, in fact, be virtually impossible to play this game without altering meanings!) Deletions that would result in ungrammatical sentences or sentences that are meaningless are, of course, not allowed by the rules of the game.

Learners should be encouraged to follow up their suggestions as to which word or words to delete with a reading of the resulting sentence(s), with appropriate stress, rhythm and intonation, so that the others can *hear* as well as see before judging whether the suggestions are acceptable.

If strips of card are used, as recommended above, it is easier to manage discussion of suggestions from the class as to which word or words might be deleted. Suggestions which prove unacceptable can be more quickly corrected – by you replacing the word strips which you have just removed – than if you used board and chalk, which might entail a good deal of rubbing out and writing in of words.

This is a cooperative game, and is judged to have come to a satisfactory end when everyone agrees that no further deletions can be made.

Example

Consider the following sentence, from a children's version of *Robinson Crusoe*:

Nearly everything in the ship was spoiled by the sea water, though I managed to save some casks of wine, a kettle, a spade, an axe, and a pair of tongs.

This sentence can be reduced in a few simple steps to:

The ship was spoiled by water. I managed to save wine and tongs.

After yet more deletions, the sentences can be further reduced to:

The ship managed.

(This last sentence is grammatically correct, although it is admittedly rather strained!)

True/false games

This is one of the great families of games. And, as in all flourishing families, there are not only many members in existence but many still to be born! Essentially, someone makes a statement which is either true or false. The game is to decide which it is. Even in this small selection of True/false games, it can be seen that all levels of proficiency can benefit from this sort of challenge.

66 Repeat it if it's true

Language	Repeating sentences after the teacher. Distinguishing true and false statements.
Skills	Listening and speaking.
Control	Controlled.
Level	Beginners.
Time	5–10 minutes.
Materials	Large pictures.

Preparation

Collect about 10–15 pictures which you can hold up and which may be seen the length of the classroom. Each picture should emphasise a single concept, e.g.

running, swimming, climbing
has got . . . hasn't got . . .
some, any
in, on, under, next to

Procedure

Class work.
 Hold up one of the pictures and make a true *or* false statement about

it. The class should listen and repeat what you have said, *if it is true.*

You can have a competition with the class. Give yourself a point every time you can get the class to repeat something which is untrue, and give the class a point when they respond correctly (by repeating something true or ignoring something false).

Teacher: He's running.
Class: He's running.
Teacher: That's one point for you.

Teacher: She's swimming.
Class:
Teacher: That's another point for you.

67   Correct me if I'm wrong

Language	Identifying mistakes, correcting mistakes, and interrupting politely, using *Excuse me, you said . . .*, *You should have said . . . instead.*
Skills	Listening, speaking and reading.
Control	Guided.
Level	All.
Time	10 minutes.
Materials	Any text which all the learners can have copies of.

Preparation

Select an appropriate text and make copies.

Procedure

Class, group or pair work.

Read out the text and deliberately change some of it.

The learners should follow their copy of the text and immediately stop you when they notice one of the changes.

Once the game is understood it can be played in groups or pairs. For example, one might read the text as, 'Read out the text and deliberately change all of it. The learners must follow . . .'

Learner: Excuse me, you said 'all' instead of 'some' and you should have said, 'The learners should follow'.

68 Don't let them pull your leg

Language	Making sentences, first in the affirmative then in the negative (*'s not, don't,* etc.).
Skills	Principally listening for detail. Speaking and writing occur in group or pair work.
Control	Free.
Level	All.
Time	15–20 minutes to prepare a text. 3–4 minutes for each learner who reads a text.
Materials	None.

Preparation

None, unless you would like to prepare your talk (see *Procedure*).

Procedure

Class, group or pair work.

Discuss the idea that there are always people who like 'to pull other people's legs', i.e. to make them look a little foolish. Explain that this game will train the learners not to have their legs pulled! Explain that you will talk and include a few untrue statements. The learners must immediately raise their hands on hearing an untrue statement and say what is wrong with it.

Once the idea of the game is understood, it can be played in groups or in pairs. Learners might prepare their 'talk' in writing, perhaps for homework.

Teacher *or* Learner 1: Yesterday I went into town and saw a marvellous car. It had six legs and went very . . .

Learner 2: That's not true. Cars don't have legs, they have wheels. And they don't have *six* wheels either.

Teacher: Oh, sorry. You are quite right. Anyway, it was going very fast indeed. I was at the chemist's buying some bread . . .

Teacher: Paris is the capital of Italy . . .

Learner 3: *Rome* is the capital of Italy!

69   Super sleuth

Language	Identifying and discussing the discrepancies between two texts, with use of the past simple.
Skills	Listening, speaking and reading.
Control	Guided.
Level	Intermediate/advanced.
Time	20–30 minutes.
Materials	Texts at an appropriate level.

Preparation

In this game, the learners study similar texts to spot the differences between them. With advanced learners, this can often be done simply by taking articles on the same topic from two different newspapers.

Alternatively, the teacher can compose one or both the texts. The texts could be, for example, the statements of two people accused of a crime, but who claim to have been together miles from the scene of the crime. The statements would contain many examples of past tenses.

Procedure

Class work.

The learners study the two texts and look for differences. In the case of the alibi example:

Learner 1: Stan says that they went to the pub at eight o'clock and Bert says they went there at 8.30.

Learner 2: Yes, and Bert says he bought the drinks, and Stan says that he bought them.

70 There's something wrong somewhere

Language	Describing pictures and identifying objects.
Skills	Reading.
Control	Guided.
Level	All.
Time	According to the length of the texts.
Materials	A picture or pictures. For class use, a slide or a large magazine picture.

Preparation

You (or the learners) must write three texts about the picture or pictures, two of which contain some errors of fact. Make copies of the texts.

Procedure

Class or group work.

Display the picture(s). Give the learners the three duplicated descriptions of the picture(s). The learners first find the description that is completely correct. They then underline all the mistakes in the others.

An extension of this would be to have two or three descriptions of the pictures, all of which contain some errors of fact. Between them, however, they provide all that is needed for a fully correct description. The learners put these bits together to produce a correct description.

71 One of them isn't telling the truth

Language	Describing pictures and identifying objects.
Skills	Principally listening.
Control	Free.
Level	All.
Time	The two learners giving the descriptions will need 20 minutes' preparation time. The actual descriptions will take only 2 or 3 minutes altogether.
Materials	A picture, perhaps of a scene, showing a number of objects and people, for each pair or group.

Preparation

Collect the pictures.

Procedure

Pair work leading to class or group work.

Give one picture to two learners. Tell them that one of them will have to describe the picture to the rest of the group or class as it really is and one will have to invent a description. This latter description may be partly accurate or totally fictitious. Give them 20 minutes to plan what to say and to write it out.

The pair now face the group or class, show them the picture, and each appears to describe the picture. The group or class must decide which description is authentic.

Note: This game, like so many others, may be adapted to needs of specialist learners: for example, the picture could be of a piece of machinery and be used by engineering students.

Memory games

Essentially, these games challenge the players' ability to remember. Surprisingly, perhaps, this simple basic challenge can lead to many different games and variations. The inevitable differences between what players remember lead to discussion, in which opinions and information are exchanged.

72 What's behind you?

Language	Listing and describing objects and places, and, in Variations 1 and 2, describing people's appearance, e.g. *There's a . . ., There are some . . ., There aren't any . . ., He/She's wearing . . .*
Skills	Listening and speaking, and, in Variation 1, reading.
Control	Free.
Level	Beginners/intermediate.
Time	2–3 minutes.
Materials	Chalkboard (optional).

Preparation

None.

Procedure

Class work.
    Tell the class not to turn round. Ask them what they think is behind them. They might list other people in the class, furniture, pictures on the walls, windows, etc. Ask for descriptions of the things they mention. You might also ask what the learners can remember of the street outside the school, e.g.
Teacher: Think about the street outside the school. What can you remember?

Learner 1: There are some trees . . .
Teacher: Yes. Are there trees on *both* sides of the street?
Learner 1: No, there aren't any on the other side.
Learner 2: No! There's one by the grocer's.

Variation 1
Class work.

Before you explain the game to the class, ask two of them to go outside the classroom. Explain the game and ask the learners to describe what the two are wearing. You could write on the board a summary of what they say. Ask the two outside to come back in and compare.

Variation 2
Pair work.

A learner is asked to close his/her eyes and describe his/her neighbour's appearance. Alternatively, the learners could stand back to back.

73   Kim's game

Language	Listing and naming objects, or pictures of objects.
	Variation 1: Numbers and plurals (e.g. *Three suitcases*).
	Variation 2: Adjectives (e.g. *A red suitcase . . . The green case is bigger . . .*).
	Variation 3: Containers (e.g. *A bottle of milk*).
	Variation 4: Present perfect (e.g. *You've put . . .*), past simple (e.g. *It was . . .*), and prepositions (e.g. *next to . . .*).
	Variation 5: Present perfect and comparatives (e.g. *You've made the tree taller*).
	Variation 6: Describing and comparing.
	Variation 7: Discussing and describing.
Skills	Listening, speaking and writing.
Control	Guided.
Level	Beginners/intermediate.
Time	5 minutes.
Materials	A collection of objects or pictures; OHP (optional); paper and pencils.

Preparation

Essentially you need a collection of small objects or pictures of objects
which you know the learners can name. Here are some of the alternative
ways of getting a collection together:
– a number (six to eight) of small objects on a table
– a number of small magazine pictures of objects on a table
– a number of small, quick sketches of objects on the board
– a number of small sketches of objects on pieces of transparency on the
  OHP.

Have a cloth or piece of paper to hide the objects or pictures. If you are
using the OHP you do not need to switch the machine off, since you can
simply cover the lens with your hand or a book.

Procedure

Class work leading to optional pair work.

Lay six to eight objects and/or pictures on the table, or display six to
eight pictures on the board. Tell the learners that you are going to
challenge their powers of observation and memory. Give the learners
20 seconds to look at the objects and/or pictures, then hide them with a
cloth or sheet of paper.

Tell the learners to write down as many names as they can remember.
Then ask them to tell you what they have written.
Teacher: What have you written?
  or: What can you remember?

Finally, remove the cloth or sheet of paper and let the learners compare
their lists with the objects and/or pictures.

Warning: Make sure that everyone can see the objects and/or pictures.

Variation 1
Class work.

NUMBERS AND PLURALS: If you want the learners to practise
numbers and plural forms, then make sure you have several objects
and/or pictures which are the same, for example three suitcases, two
cameras and one typewriter.

Variation 2
Class work.

ADJECTIVES: To enable the learners to use adjectives, have several objects and/or pictures which are of the same kind but are of different colour, size shape, etc. For example, include a red, a black and a green suitcase. This can give excellent practice in the use of comparatives, e.g. 'The green case is a bit bigger than the black case and it's about the same size as the red case'.

Variation 3
Class work.

CONTAINERS: Use, for example, a bottle of milk, a box of matches, a tin of soup, a packet of soap powder, a bag of apples and a tube of toothpaste.

Variation 4
Class work.

PRESENT PERFECT, PAST SIMPLE, PREPOSITIONS: This variation of the game usually works better with real objects than with pictures. Remember that 'real' objects may include Cuisenaire rods or toys, such as a plane, car or bridge. Place six to eight objects on a table. Make sure that several of them are positioned, for example, on top of / underneath / next to / inside other objects.
After 20 seconds, ask the learners to look away. Change the position of one of the objects.
Teacher: What have I done?
Learner: You've put the tape underneath the dictionary.
Teacher: And where was it?
Learner: It was next to the watch.

Variation 5
Class work leading to pair work.

PRESENT PERFECT AND COMPARATIVES: Instead of using objects or prepared pictures ask a number of learners to draw some simple objects on the OHP or the board. (This in itself will provide a rich language situation!) Some of the objects might have colour on them.
Tell the learners to close their eyes and to put their heads on their arms whilst you, or a learner, *change* some of the drawings making them longer or shorter, fatter, taller, redder, greener, etc. Challenge the class to tell you what you have done, e.g.
Teacher: What have I done?
Learner: You've made the tree taller.
   or: The tree is taller.

The learners can play the same game in pairs using paper, pencil and rubber.

Variation 6
Individual work leading to pair work.

DESCRIBING AND COMPARING: For more advanced students, you may show them about 15 objects or pictures of objects and then ask them to write down what they remember, *describing the objects* in detail. It is easier and equally challenging to show the objects or pictures *one after the other* instead of at the same time.

When the learners have written down everything they can remember, they should exchange their writing with their neighbours. Each learner marks his/her neighbour's work as you hold up the objects and pictures again.

As you hold up each object, discuss with the class its character, e.g.

Teacher: What's this?
Learner 1: A scarf.
Teacher: Did John remember it?
Learner 1: Yes, he did.
Teacher: What did he say about it?
            How did he describe it?
Learner 1: He said (*reading from his partner's work*) it was red, green, yellow . . . and woolly.
Teacher: Well! Is it? Was he right?
Learner 2: No, he wasn't.
            It isn't red, it's orange!
Teacher: Well, it's sort of red, isn't it?
Learner 3: And it isn't green.
Teacher: Tell me when John was right and when he was wrong.
Learner 4: He was right when he said that the scarf is (was) red, yellow and woolly, and wrong when he said that it is (was) green.

Variation 7
Group work.
DISCUSSING AND DESCRIBING: An alternative and more elaborate way of organising a memory game of this kind is as follows.

Divide the class into an even number of groups. Give each group a number of either magazine pictures or objects (the pictures should not be of a general scene but rather highlight an object or person).

First of all the group should examine and discuss their pictures (or objects). Then the pictures should be turned face down (or the objects covered) and the group should compile a description from memory of each one.

Then each group must work with another group. They should exchange pictures and test each other's memory.

74   Pass the message

Language	Repeating whole sentences.
Skills	All.
Control	Controlled, and, for advanced students, free.
Level	All.
Time	10–15 minutes for the discussion at the end of the game, or longer with advanced students. The game itself can be played while other work is going on.
Materials	Each learner should have a pen and a piece of paper.

Preparation

Prepare a message before the lesson. Here are some examples for different levels of learners, e.g.

57394
My black, heavy bag is under the bush.
I will be waiting for you just outside the swing doors of the Green Pig at a quarter to nine.

You might first consider discussing the prevalent and destructive nature of rumour with the class. Then introduce this game as an example of how difficult it is to report things accurately.

Procedure

Class work.

Show the sentence you have prepared to someone sitting at the front and to one side. Let this player see the sentence for five seconds, then take it from him/her and keep it yourself. That first player must then write the sentence he/she remembers on a piece of paper and show it to his/her neighbour for five seconds. The neighbour does the same until the message, usually much changed, has gone round the class.

Throughout this part of the game you can carry on with your normal lesson.

When you see that the message has reached the last person, ask him/her to read out what he/she has written down. There will probably be cries of astonishment!

Then read out the message as it began.

Now ask all the learners in turn to read out the message *they* passed on.

If you want to get some intensive language work out of the game, particularly for advanced students, discuss why each of the changes might have been made. Are they changes which don't change the sense significantly? Are the changes grammatically wrong? Making a detailed analysis of these changes can be a very subtle and informative activity.

Variation 1
Class work.

More stress can be given to listening and speaking if the message is *whispered* to the neighbour. This can be done as a race. Different teams 'pass' the same message which you whisper to the learners at the front of each team or row. The player at the end acts appropriately, e.g.

Open a window, please.
Please give me a black pencil.
Would you please draw a square on the blackboard.

Variation 2
Class work.

Instead of attempting to pass on the message received, each player should deliberately distort it in some way with the aim of creating an outrageous rumour. Otherwise the same procedure applies as above.

Variation 3
Class work.

A short story or joke is whispered, not just a sentence.

75   Pass the picture

Language	Too (*short, fat,* etc.) and *not* (*long, thin,* etc.) *enough* occur in this activity. Also the vocabulary of the picture which is being passed on.
Skills	Listening and speaking.
Control	Free.
Level	Intermediate/advanced.
Time	10–15 minutes for the discussion at the end of the game. (The game itself can be played while other work is going on.)
Materials	Each learner should have a black felt-tip pen and a piece of paper.

Preparation

Draw a simple picture on a piece of paper before the lesson. (See, for example, the illustration.)

Note: The drawings must be big enough to be seen by the whole class when displayed for discussion.

Procedure

Class work.

Show the picture you have prepared to someone sitting at the front and to one side. Let them see the picture for ten seconds, then take it back and keep it. The first player must then draw the picture as he/she remembers it. Then he/she must show it to his/her neighbour for ten seconds and so on until everyone has passed on *their* version of the picture their neighbour showed them. Throughout this part of the game you should carry on with your normal lesson.

Display the last picture and the first one together and discuss the differences. Then ask people to stand up in threes or fours showing the way the picture was modified as it passed through the class. Discuss the changes. Finally, if possible, display *all* the pictures, in order, on the wall.

76 Pelmanism

Language	Making comments about the Pelmanism cards provided, and agreeing and disagreeing politely (e.g. *I'm sorry I don't . . .*). In Variation 2, the learners use *I've got . . ., Have you got . . .? What have you got . . .?*
Skills	Listening, speaking and reading.
Control	Guided.
Level	All learners will enjoy playing this game, although Variation 2 is most useful for beginners/intermediate learners.
Time	10–15 minutes, except for Variation 2, which takes 5–10 minutes.
Materials	Sets of cards (see *Preparation*).

Preparation

Prepare a set of 20 matching cards for each group of four to five players. Alternatively, the learners can produce the cards.

In each set, there are ten pairs of cards: the pairs can relate to each other in a range of ways, according to the language needs of the learners, e.g.

On one card the picture of an invention and on the other the date it was invented.

On one card a photo (from a magazine) of a person, object or scene and on the other a written description of it.

On one card is written a statement and an invitation to the learner to find a response which he/she could use to agree, disagree politely, partly agree, etc.; on the other card is the response he needs.

Procedure

Group work.

The learners, in groups of four to five, lay the cards in neat rows face down so that the pictures and writing on the cards cannot be seen. One player then picks up two of the cards. If he/she thinks they match, he/she makes some appropriate comment to the others, e.g.

Aspirin was invented in 1853.
This car is green and it is made in France.

To disagree politely a learner could say, 'I'm sorry I don't agree with that, I think that . . .'

If the other players agree, he/she keeps the two cards and can pick up two more.

When two cards are picked up which do not match, they must be shown to the other players and replaced in exactly the same position from which they were taken. Then the next player has a turn.

This continues until the cards have been paired off. The player with the most pairs is the winner.

Further examples for the cards:

– words and their definitions
– maps of countries (from travel brochures) and the name of the country
– coins or stamps and the name of their country of origin
– titles of books or quotations and their authors
– pictures of different fish, trees, birds, flowers, etc. and their names
– photographs and matching dialogues
– cartoons and their captions (cut from comics, etc.)
– riddles and their solutions
– questions and answers

Variation 1
Individual or pair work.

To allow the learners to become accustomed to the cards and thus reduce the chances of too much argument later, they could play with the cards individually, or in pairs, before using them to play Pelmanism. They could time themselves to see how quickly they match all the cards.

This is particularly beneficial as a means of keeping usefully occupied those learners who finish a piece of work before the others.

It is a good idea to keep sets of these cards always available for such situations.

Variation 2
Group work.

Give one card to each player. The players then look at their cards and try to find who has the matching card by asking other learners, e.g.

I've got a picture of the Canadian flag. What have you got?
Have you got the card that goes with this?

77 Would you make a good witness?

Language	Describing people's appearance and actions, using the past continuous (e.g. *He was standing at a bus stop . . .*). In Variation 1, the vocabulary for naming and describing clothing is used. In Variation 2, the past simple is also used (e.g. *He came into the room*).
Skills	Listening and speaking.
Control	Free
Level	Intermediate/advanced.
Time	10–15 minutes.
Materials	A picture of a busy street scene. In the variations, a collection of clothing and objects.

Preparation

Select the picture. Sources for such a picture include magazines, tourist publicity, road safety publicity and tourist slides. Ideally, the picture should be big enough to be seen from the back of the class but this is not essential.

Procedure

Class work.

Before showing the picture, ask if any of the learners have witnessed an accident or crime in the street. Discuss with the class the difficulties of being a witness. Then tell them that you are going to show them a picture of a street for a few seconds and that they must try to remember as much of it as they can.

If the picture is big, show it from the front of the class. If it is small, walk slowly about the class, letting the learners look at it as you pass.

Hide the picture and ask the learners to tell you what they saw. You may have to prompt the learners or cross-check their answers, e.g.

Teacher: What did you see in the picture? What can you remember?
Learner 1: A man . . .
Teacher: Yes. What was he doing?
Learner 1: He was standing at a bus stop.
Teacher: Was anyone else standing at the bus stop?
Learner 2: Yes, a boy.
Teacher: Can you tell me what he was wearing?
Learner 2: He was wearing a T-shirt and jeans.
Teacher: *Was* he wearing a T-shirt?
Learner 3: No, I think it was a jersey.

Finally, show the picture to the class again.

Warning: In case the learners find difficulty in talking about the picture, have a number of questions ready.

Variation 1
Class and group work.

Give each group a picture, e.g. a scene including objects and people. They must prepare 10–15 questions on this picture.

Then ask one learner to show his/her group's picture to another group for about 30 seconds.

Then *either* the two groups join together and the first group ask their questions: *or* the learners pair off, one from each group. The learner from the group which has just shown their picture asks the questions.

Variation 2
Class work.

To give the learners practice in describing articles of clothing, make a collection of hats, scarves, glasses, coats, etc. Ask one learner to dress up in some of these clothes *outside* the classroom. He/she should then come into the classroom for a few seconds, before going out again. The class must try to describe his/her appearance.

Variation 3
Class work.

To give practice in the description of clothing and objects and in the use of the past simple and the past continuous, you might like to arrange for a smash-and-grab raid in the classroom!

Before the lesson starts, explain your plan to two learners. They should dress up in strange clothes, enter the classroom, seize a variety of objects, putting some into a bag, others into their pockets and carrying the remainder. They should then leave the classroom. The whole 'crime' should not take more than a few seconds.

The two 'criminals' should make sure that everyone can see what they are doing so, for example, they should not turn their backs on the class.

Ask the class to describe the 'criminals'' appearance, what they did and which objects they took.

Question and answer games

As with any grammatical point, there is often a danger in foreign-language learning that practice of question-forming becomes detached for too long from real use, e.g. making enquiries. We have included in this section a variety of games designed to create contexts in which the learners *want* to ask questions in order to find something out, for example, *General knowledge quiz.*

Sometimes, however, there is a role for more mechanical practice of question forms – as the rock climber needs to do press-ups! We believe that even here amusing and challenging contexts will lead to more efficient learning, as in, for example, *Distractions.*

78 Don't say 'Yes' or 'No'

Language	Asking questions and giving answers, especially asking questions with question tags (e.g. . . ., *isn't it?* . . ., *don't you?* . . ., *do you?*) and giving complete phrases for answers. Using *of course, of course not, perhaps, clearly, obviously, I'm sure, I've no idea.*
Skills	Listening and speaking.
Control	Guided.
Level	Intermediate/advanced.
Time	5–10 minutes.
Materials	None.

Preparation

None.

Procedure

Class work leading to group or pair work.

This can be a team competition. Put a number of questions to each team. Each question must be answered without delay and without the use of either 'Yes', or 'No'. The team which answers the most questions in this way wins.

The teacher asks questions of this type:

Your name is Peter, isn't it?
You do live near the school, don't you?
You don't come to school by bus, do you?
You didn't do your homework last night, did you?
It was raining at nine o'clock this morning, wasn't it?

The learners should reply, e.g.

Not at all, my name is Ann.
Not quite, my home is a long way from school.
Indeed I do.
I certainly did.
I don't think so.

When the learners have seen how the game works, they can fire questions at each other to try to catch each other out.

Warning: Make sure that the learners are already familiar with the more usual responses beginning with 'Yes' or 'No'. Of course, the learners should also be clear about the various alternative responses. These might be written on the board.

79 Half the class knows

Language	Asking questions and giving answers, with expressions such as *not exactly* . . .
Skills	Listening and speaking.
Control	Free.
Level	All.
Time:	5–10 minutes.
Materials	Pictures or line drawings.

Preparation

For class work you should have three to six pictures of magazine page size. They should not be too detailed. Stickmen drawings are ideal but simple photographs are also suitable. See examples on p. 154. For pair or group work you will need three to six pictures for each pair or group.

Procedure

Class work leading to group or pair work.

You or a learner or a group of learners look at a picture which the rest of the class cannot see. (This is an opportunity to involve a less able learner in the key role.) The ones who cannot see must ask questions to find out what is in the picture.

The game may be played at a variety of levels. At the simplest level, you may say there is a man in the picture and ask, e.g.

Teacher: What is he doing?
Class: Is he running?
Teacher: No.
Class: Is he swimming?

At a more advanced level, you may use a more complicated picture and give no clue concerning the content of it, e.g.

Class: Is it inside?
Teacher: No, not exactly.
Class: Outside?
Teacher: Well . . . yes, but partly inside.
Class: Is it a door?

80 Test your knowledge

Language	Any questions of fact, and answers to them.
Skills	Reading.
Control	Controlled.
Level	Intermediate/advanced.
Time	10–20 minutes.
Materials	Pieces of paper or card.

Preparation

Cut out at least 20 pieces of paper or card, about 5 cm × 10 cm, for each
learner or pair of learners. Dividing these into pairs, write a question on
one of the cards and the appropriate answer on the other. (The learners
themselves could be asked to help by copying duplicate sets of cards to
ensure that there are enough to go round the whole class.)
Here are three types of subject with a few examples:

General knowledge

Where is the Taj Mahal?	It's in India.
Where was Tolstoy born?	In Russia.
What is the capital of Scotland?	Edinburgh.
How many players are there in a cricket team?	Eleven.
Who painted 'Guernica'?	Picasso.

Jokes

Which king of England wore the largest shoes?	The one with the largest feet.
What can you have when someone has taken it?	A photograph.
What is the difference between a nail and a bad boxer?	One is knocked in, the other is knocked out.
Waiter, there is a dead fly in my soup!	Yes, sir, it's the hot water which has killed it.

Cause and effect

What would happen if the sun lost its heat?	All living things would die.
What would happen if we didn't eat for a long time?	We would die.
What happens when we add blue to yellow?	It turns green
What happens if we boil an egg for six minutes?	It becomes hard.

Procedure

Pair/individual work.

The learners should exchange sets of cards with each other once they
have prepared them. Explain that the questions must be paired with the
appropriate answers.

Variation
Pair/individual work.
Sentences are divided into two parts. Each part is written on a separate card. Learners must sort out the cards and put the correct pairs together.

81   Twenty questions

Language	Asking questions to acquire information.
Skills	Listening and speaking.
Control	Free.
Level	Intermediate/advanced.
Time	15 minutes.
Materials	None.

Preparation

None.

Procedure

Class work.
There are many versions of this game. A common version was played regularly on BBC radio. In this, the question-master thinks of something and simply tells the players whether it is 'animal, vegetable, mineral or abstract'. The players can then put 20 questions to the question-master to discover what he is thinking of. Traditionally, the questions are put so that they can be answered by 'Yes' or 'No'. The teacher may, of course, limit the choice, for example, to everyday objects, pets, professions, verbs, phrases, famous people and where they live.
If a learner acts as the question-master, you have the opportunity of helping the class by asking a few questions which narrow down the range of possibilities, e.g.

Is it bigger/smaller than a car?
Can you eat it?
Have you got one?

Would you normally find one in a house?
Is it made of wood?
Can it be easily broken?

If the players discover what it is in less than 20 questions, they win a point. If they do not, the question-master scores a point.

Variation 1
Class work.
　You can give part of a simple story to the class and they can try to find out more, or complete the story, in 20 questions.

Variation 2
Class work.
　The teacher, or a learner, pretends that he/she is a famous person, dead or alive, or that he/she lives in a well-known city. The players can ask 20 questions to try to discover who, or where, the questioner is.

Variation 3
Class work.
　A learner thinks of a profession and writes it down. The class have 20 questions to find the answer.

Variation 4
Class work.
　A learner says, 'I've got an interesting pet' and the others ask, 'Has it got four legs?', 'Can it fly?' etc., until the correct answer is guessed. If a learner receives the answer 'Yes', he/she is allowed a further question.

Variation 5
Class or group work.
　One person in the class, or in a group of learners, imagines where he/she might be hiding, and the others must ask questions to try and find out. The location might be restricted to a picture, or to a place which all the learners know. The person pretending to hide might even choose to say that he/she is an insect or other small creature. This would demand a very precise location!

82   General knowledge quiz

Language	Wh– questions, agreeing, disagreeing; speculating, expressing doubt, ignorance, e.g. *Yes, I think you're right . . ., Would I be right in thinking . . .?*
Skills	Listening and speaking.
Control	Free.
Level	Intermediate/advanced.
Time	10–15 minutes.
Materials	Reference books (optional).

Preparation

The quiz can cover a range of topics, or can concentrate on one area. It is important that none of the learners should know the answers to all the questions, so that the speculation and argument are real and so that the learners acquire some new information through the foreign language. An excellent source for such quizzes is *The Guinness Book of Records*. This may suggest, in particular, quizzes using superlatives and comparatives. The following quiz examples would give practice in the use of past tenses.

1   Who first sailed alone around the world?
   a) Sir Francis Drake
   b) Sir Francis Chichester
   c) *Joshua Slocum*
   d) Christopher Columbus

2   Who first flew alone across the Atlantic?
   a) *Charles Lindberg*
   b) The Wright brothers
   c) Alexander Fleming
   d) Louis Pasteur

3   Who produced the first television picture?
   a) *The Scotsman, John Baird*
   b) The American, Neil Armstrong
   c) The Russian, Yuri Gagarin
   d) The Englishman, George Stephenson

The following examples give practice in the use and understanding of wh– questions.

1 Where is the Eiffel Tower?
2 Where was Shakespeare born?
3 Who is the American president?
4 Who wrote *Robinson Crusoe*?
5 What are the colours of the British flag?
6 What is the capital of Italy?
7 How many players are there in a football team?
8 How does the petrol engine work?
9 Which is the longest river in the world?
10 In which countries does the elephant live?

Procedure

Class work.

When a learner first hazards a guess, e.g. 'Was it Sir Francis Drake who first sailed alone around the world?' the teacher should neither confirm nor correct the answer. He/she should rather use it to stimulate others to agree or disagree, e.g.

Do you agree with that?
What do you think?
Does anyone disagree?
Does everyone agree?

Only after a good deal of discussion should the teacher say which is the correct answer. He/she could then use the incorrect answers to stimulate more discussion, e.g.

What did Sir Francis Drake / Christopher Columbus do?
Why was Louis Pasteur famous?

The teacher can act as a model, reminding the learners of the sorts of expressions they can use in such a situation, e.g.

Would I be right in thinking that . . .?
Did he, by any chance . . .?
Yes, I think you're right when you say . . ., but . . .
No, I don't think that can be right, because . . .

83   What were you doing last night?

Language	Asking questions (*Who . . .? Did . . .?* etc.).
Skills	Listening and speaking.
Control	Free.
Level	Intermediate/advanced.
Time	10–15 minutes.
Materials	None.

Preparation

None.

Procedure

Class work.

Make a statement and explain that the learners should question you about it, e.g.

Teacher: I saw an old friend last night.
Learner 1: Where did you see him?
Teacher: He came to my house.
Learner 2: Did you have dinner?
Teacher: Yes.
Learner 3: Who cooked the dinner?
Teacher: I did.
Learner 4: What did you cook?

A more gamelike quality will emerge if you create a fantasy, e.g.

Teacher: I saw a green man last night.
Learner 1: Where?
Teacher: He was on a train.
Learner 2: What was he doing?
Teacher: Talking.
Learner 3: Who was he talking to?
Teacher: A small, silver dog.
Learner 4: Did he speak in English?
Teacher: Yes.

Other opening statements might be:

My friend has just bought a new car.
My neighbours had a quarrel last night.
My great-grandfather has just had a marvellous holiday.
I've got a wonderful parrot.

84   Who are you?

Language	Questions and answers to establish people's appearance, interests and other details.
Skills	All.
Control	Free.
Level	Intermediate/advanced.
Time	60–80 minutes.
Materials	Each learner should have a piece of paper or card about 20 cm × 30 cm; for the variation, a picture showing at least four people will be required for each group.

Preparation

Cut cards to size. For the variation, select suitable pictures..

Procedure

Individual work leading to class work and pair work.
   This game or activity is divided into three stages:
1 *Each learner makes a 'biographical card' of a well-known person*
   The illustration and writing should be on one side only. The
   following information might be included: appearance (including a
   photograph or drawing), verbal description, age, family, job
   (including a few details), other interests, hobbies, etc.
2 *All these biographical cards are displayed*
   All the learners study the cards on display and write down the names.
   They must try to remember the information.
3 *Learners work in pairs*
   Give each learner one of the biographical cards, not necessarily the
   one he/she made. Then, working in pairs, the learners question each

other to find out who the other is. The only rule is that the name should not be asked for. Each learner is then allowed one guess at the name on the other learner's biographical card.

Variation
Group work.
Each group of learners has a magazine picture or photograph showing at least four people. One learner in the group thinks of one of the people in the picture or photograph but does not tell the other learners who it is. They must question him/her to find out which it is. You may decide to limit the number of questions that may be asked.

85 Flipping

Language	Asking questions, using a nonsense word as a verb in a variety of forms; giving answers.
Skills	Listening and speaking.
Control	Free.
Level	Intermediate/advanced.
Time	5 minutes or more.
Materials	None.

Preparation

None.

Procedure

Class work and group work.
One learner comes to the front of the class and thinks of a verb of action. He/she tells you, but not the rest of the class, what the verb is. The rest of the class must try and find out by asking questions, substituting the word 'flip' for the 'mystery' verb in all the questions, e.g.
Learner 2: Have you ever flipped?
Learner 1: Yes.
Learner 3: Is flipping enjoyable?
Learner 1: It can be.

Learner 4: Is flipping a sport?
Learner 1: No, not exactly. It could be called a hobby or pastime.
Learner 5: When did you flip last?
Learner 1: This morning.
Learner 6: Where were you when you flipped?
Learner 1: In the bathroom.
Learner 7: Were you doing anything else at the same time as you were flipping?
Learner 1: Yes, having a shower.
Learner 8: You were singing.
Learner 1: Yes!

As soon as the learners are familiar with the game, encourage them to play it in groups, so that more of them have an opportunity to speak.

86 Avoidance

Language	Asking questions and giving answers, avoiding use of a given word.
Skills	Listening and speaking.
Control	Free.
Level	Intermediate/advanced.
Time	5 minutes, or more.
Materials	None.

Preparation

None.

Procedure

Class work and group work.
   One learner comes to the front of the class, and, without telling the other learners, decides on a 'mystery' word. You may restrict the choice, if you like, to a particular topic area. By questioning, the rest of the class must try and find out what the word is. The learner at the front must answer all questions put to him/her, and answer them fully and fairly.

The only constraint is that he/she must avoid using the 'mystery' word in the answers given.

As soon as the learners are familiar with the game, encourage them to play it in groups, so that more of them have an opportunity to speak.

87 Alibis

Language	Asking questions, giving answers, and narrating past events. Many question forms are practised: *Where . . .? Who . . .? Why . . .? Did . . .?* etc.
Skills	Listening and speaking.
Control	Free.
Level	Intermediate/advanced.
Time	30 minutes for the learners to prepare an alibi, and 10–15 minutes to play.
Materials	None, except for the variation, which requires a series of action pictures.

Preparation

None.

Procedure

Pair work leading to class work.

Each pair imagine that they have to create an alibi for a given evening. They work together to produce a story which accounts for every minute between 7 p.m. and 10 p.m. on that evening. They then try to memorise the story. This preparation can take place outside the classroom, if wished.

When the alibi has been prepared, one of the two who have prepared it waits outside while the other faces the rest of the class. The class question him/her at length to find out the details of the alibi. Then his/her partner comes in and is subjected to a similar interrogation. The class try to find inconsistencies in the stories and look for contradictions. If they find any, the alibi is broken and the class win. If not, the two who made up the alibi win.

Many question forms will be used, e.g.

Learners: Where were you at 7.15?
Who else was there?
What time did you leave?
What did you do next?
Why did you go there?
Whose idea was it to go there?
How much did it cost?
Who paid?
Did you get any change?
When did you leave?
How did you get home?

Variation
Group work.

For this game you will require five pictures of actions for each group, including one showing a murder taking place! These can be very simple stickmen drawings duplicated and cut up. They could be made by the learners.

The learners work in groups of five. Each player takes one picture at random and does not show the others. Each player says what he/she was doing at eight o'clock the previous evening. The 'murderer' *invents* what he/she was doing, i.e. he/she does not base his/her statement on his/her picture. Any player may cross question another.

When everyone has said what they were doing and the cross questioning is finished, each player says who he/she thinks is the murderer. Then the murderer confesses!

Note: You may like to insist that one player always asks the next player, 'What were you doing yesterday evening?'

88 Distractions

Language	Asking questions, with emphasis on fluency.
Skills	Listening and speaking.
Control	Free.
Level	All.
Time	2–3 minutes, or more.
Materials	Whatever is appropriate to the task (see *Procedure*).

Preparation

None.

Procedure

Class work or group work.

One learner is given a silent task to do, e.g. copying a short paragraph from a book, doing an arithmetical calculation, sorting a number of coins according to date. The other learners must try to prevent him/her from completing – or, if possible, even from starting – the task. This they do by asking questions. Whenever a question is asked, the first learner must stop what he/she is doing, and may only resume the task when there is a momentary silence (if any) between questions, or when the flow of questions eventually dries up (if at all).

Variation
Class work or group work.

Once the class is familiar with the game, you may, for variety's sake, alter the rules slightly: the learner who has been given the task to do should continue as best he/she can even while the others are asking their questions. The object is to see how quickly the learner can complete the task despite the distractions!

89   Questions for answers

Language	Making up suitable questions to accompany given answers.
Skills	All.
Control	Guided.
Level	All.
Time	10 minutes or more.
Materials	Chalkboard. In the variation, slips of paper.

Preparation

Write a number of statements on the board which are answers – or possible answers – to questions, but do *not* communicate those questions to the class. The statements may be chosen at random, or they may be related to a given topic. (Note, however, that in the variation the statements *and* the corresponding questions are written on slips of paper, not on the board.)

Procedure

Individual or pair work, leading to class work.

Give the learners, either as individuals or working in pairs, a few minutes to look at the statements which you have written on the board, and to write down questions to which they think the statements would make appropriate answers. Consider all the learners' questions as a class, and decide which seem to be the most appropriate.

Variation
Class work.

Write a set of questions *and* a corresponding set of matching answers. Write them all on separate slips of paper. Shuffle all the questions and all the answers together. Give one slip only to each learner, at random. The learners should then move round the classroom reading out whatever question (or answer) is on their slip, trying to find the person who has the matching answer (or question).

Guessing and speculating games

Essentially, in guessing and speculating games, someone knows something and the others must find out what it is. There are many games and variations in this section, all based on this simple idea. It is possible to play many of them by making short unconnected guesses. Played in this way, the games are useful for the less sophisticated learner and/or the learner whose English is limited. However, learners with a wider range of English at their command should be required to think and speak in a more extended, connected way.

In most of the games described here the majority of the class or group are 'guessers' rather than 'knowers'. Organised this way round, more work is done by the majority!

90   Hiding and finding

Language	Asking questions, using *Is it* + preposition + place (e.g. *Is it on top of the cupboard?*). Making suggestions, using *Let's* + verb + object + preposition + place (e.g. *Let's hide the watch on top of the cupboard*). In Variations 1: *Have you hidden it . . .?* In Variation 2: *Is it hidden . . .?* or *Has it been hidden . . .?*
Skills	Listening and speaking.
Control	Guided.
Level	Beginners, and in Variations 1 and 2, intermediate.
Time	15 minutes.
Materials	A small object which can be hidden.

Preparation

None.

Procedure

Class work.

One or two learners should be sent outside the room. The class then discuss what small object they would like to hide and where it should be hidden, e.g.

Class: Let's hide this watch.
        Let's hide this coin.

        Let's hide it under the box of chalk.
        Let's hide it inside the cupboard on a shelf.

When the object is hidden, call the learner(s) in and tell him/her/them to find the object by asking questions, e.g.

Learner 1: Is it at the front of the room?
Class: Yes.
Learner 1: Is it on top of the cupboard?
Class: No . . .

Variation 1
Class work.

At an intermediate level, the learner(s) who went outside the classroom can be asked to use the present perfect:
Learner 1: Have you hidden it near the door?

Variation 2
Class work.

One or two learners go out of the classroom but only *half* the class should be responsible for choosing and hiding the object. This gives some justification for the use of the passive form if it is the *other* half of the class which is asked the questions:
Learner 1: Is it hidden at the back of the classroom?
     or: Has it been hidden at the back of the classroom?

91 Feel and think

Language	Asking questions and giving answers, naming objects, expressing doubt, e.g. *I think it's a . . . It could be a . . . I'm not sure . . .*
Skills	Listening and speaking.
Control	Guided.
Level	Beginners/intermediate, or advanced in Variation 1.
Time	2–3 minutes to demonstrate the game to the class. Another 10 minutes or more for pair work.
Materials	A collection of objects and a cloth to cover them with; in Variation 2, a blindfold and/or a bag.

Preparation

Collect about ten small objects of different shapes and sizes. A piece of cloth, a thin towel, a headscarf, or a large handkerchief will be required. It must be large enough to cover four or five of the objects.

Procedure

Class work leading to optional pair work.

Make sure that the learners know the names of at least the majority of the objects which you have collected.

Put four or five of the objects under the cloth on a table without the class seeing which ones you have chosen.

Ask a learner to feel one of the objects through the cloth and to tell you what he/she thinks it is. If correct, let the learner remove the object. Ask other learners to do the same for the other objects.

The language in this game can be restricted, e.g.
Teacher: What is it?
Learner: It's a . . .

Any of the following language might be used according to your wishes:
Teacher: What do you think it is?
Learner: I think it's a . . .
It could be a . . .
I'm not sure . . .
I don't know . . .

I know what it is but I don't know what it's called.
I know what it's called in (Swedish) but I don't know what it's
called in English.

If you think that the learners, divided into pairs, can collect a sufficient
number of objects, you will find the game easy to arrange for pair work.

Variation 1
Class work leading to optional pair work.
   Advanced learners might be asked to talk about each feature of the
object they are feeling in such a way that the rest of the class can identify
it. This will require the use of descriptive terms and the language of
speculation, e.g.
Learner 1: It's hard.
Learner 2: What's it made of?
Learner 1: I think it's made of metal.
Learner 3: What shape is it?
Learner 1: It's got two round bits. You can put your fingers through
              them. It's got two long bits which are sharp.
Learner 4: Is it a pair of scissors?
Learner 1: Yes, I think so.

Variation 2
Group or class work.
   One learner is blindfolded. He/she sits in the centre of a circle, and
one of the other learners places an object (or objects) in his/her hands,
and asks:
Learner: What is it/are they?
            Who does it/do they belong to?

That is to say, the first person must identify both the object(s) and the
owner. If this is done correctly, the two players change places. If not,
another object, belonging to a third person, is placed in the first person's
hands, and the game goes on as before.

Note: The 'feel it' game may also be played by placing the 'mystery'
objects in a bag, into which a learner dips his/her hand, and tries to
identify the objects by touch.

92   One idea at a time

Language	Describing things using adjectives.
	Variation 1: adverbs (e.g. *noisily*) and imperatives (e.g. *open, close.*
	Variation 2: names of jobs, and questions.
	Variation 3: present continuous (e.g. *You're carrying something*).
	Variation 4: present perfect (e.g. *Have you hurt . . .?*).
Skills	Listening and speaking.
Control	Guided.
Level	Beginners/intermediate.
Time	10–15 minutes.
Materials	None.

Preparation

None.

Procedure

Class work.

One learner mimes an adjective and the others try to guess what he/she is miming, e.g.

Learner 1:   Are you tired?
Mimer: (*Shakes head.*)
Learner 2:   Are you lazy?
Mimer: (*Shakes head.*)
Learner 3:   Are you bored?
Mimer: (*Nods head.*)

You should then encourage the other learners to find the reason for his/her boredom, e.g.

Learner 4:   Are you bored because you have nothing to do?

Other examples: miserable, busy, thirsty, frightened, surprised, angry.

⟫→

Variation 1
Class work.

ADVERBS AND IMPERATIVES: One learner chooses an adverb which will be easy to demonstrate, whatever action he/she is asked to do. The class then ask him/her to perform various actions and try to guess the adverb he/she has chosen.
For example, he/she may have chosen 'angrily'.
Class: Open and close the door.
Mimer: (*Opens and closes door angrily.*)
Class: Noisily!
Mimer: (*Shakes head.*)
Class: Walk to the teacher's desk.
Mimer: (*Walks angrily.*)
Class: Quickly!
Mimer: (*Shakes head.*)

Variation 2
Class work.

JOBS AND QUESTIONS: One learner mimes a job. The others try to find out what it is by asking not more than 20 questions. The mimer may only shake or nod his/her head.

Variation 3
Class work.

PRESENT CONTINUOUS: One learner mimes a sequence of actions. The others try to guess what he/she is doing. The learner who is miming must nod or shake his/her head as the class make their guesses, e.g.
Class: You're carrying something.
Mimer: (*Nods head.*)
Class: Is it a gun?
Mimer: (*Shakes head.*)
Class: Is it a stick?
Mimer: (*Nods head.*)
Class: You're climbing on to something.

Variation 4
Class work.

PRESENT PERFECT: One learner mimes an action which implies that something else has happened. The others try to guess what it is, e.g.
Mimer: (*Holds his/her thumb with an expression of pain.*)

Class: Have you hurt your thumb?
Mimer: (*Nods head.*)
Class: Have you hit it?
Mimer: (*Nods head.*)
Class: Have you hit it with a hammer?
Mimer: (*Shakes head.*)

93   Picture out of focus

Language	Describing a picture, using language items indicating uncertainty, e.g. *It might be . . . It could be . . .*
Skills	Listening and speaking.
Control	Free.
Level	Intermediate/advanced.
Time	10–15 minutes.
Materials	A slide projector and a slide. An OHP and transparency of a picture would also work but would not provide the same subtlety of colour.

Preparation

Select a slide and set up the projector.

Procedure

Class work.
   Put the slide into the projector and turn the lens out of focus *before* you switch on.
Teacher: What can you see?
Learner: Nothing.
Teacher: Nothing?
Learner: Some colours.

Ask the learners to describe what they see and to speculate about what the colours and indistinct shapes might be.

Bring the slide into focus, stopping perhaps three or four times to allow people to put forward new conjectures, e.g.

Learner 1: I think those are people on the left and that square thing above them might be a window.

Learner 2: It *could* be a picture.

Finally, bring the slide into sharp focus.

94 Box

Language	Naming and describing objects, identifying objects from their descriptions, using nouns (e.g. *comb*, *watch*), adjectives (e.g. *silver*), possessives (e.g. *my*, *mine*, *John's*). In the variation, *Have you got a . . .?* is used.
Skills	Listening and speaking.
Control	Free.
Level	All.
Time	5 minutes.
Materials	Any large box or bag.

Preparation

Ensure that a variety of small objects which the learners can name are in the classroom. You could keep small objects in your pocket and use that instead of a box or bag.

Procedure

Class work.

Go round the classroom picking up about ten small objects. Ask the learners to name each object before you put it into the box or bag.

Put your hand into the box, take hold of one of the objects but do not take it out.

Teacher: What have I got in my hand?

Learner 1: A comb.

    or: The comb.

Teacher: No.

Learner 2: A watch.
    or: The watch.
Teacher: Yes.

At this point, walk towards the learner who has guessed correctly to give him/her the object. If any other learner can say anything true about the object, he/she must call it out immediately. Walk towards that learner to give him/her the object. Again, other learners may attempt to 'win' the object by calling out a true statement.
Learner 3: It's a silver watch.
Learner 4: It's fast.
Learner 5: It's ticking.
Learner 6: It's not Big Ben.
Learner 7: It's like a person. It has a face and two hands.

When the game is over, make use of possessive forms in returning the objects to their owners.
Teacher: Whose in this?
Learner: It's mine/his/John's, etc.

Variation
Class work.
   The learners may guess what is in the box by asking the question 'Have you got a . . .?'

95 What on earth is he talking about?

Language	Describing things, people, settings and their relationships, using any appropriate complete sentence.
Skills	All.
Control	Free.
Level	All.
Time	10–20 minutes for written preparation. 5–10 minutes for listening and speaking in pairs.
Materials	Chalkboard (optional).

Preparation

Prepare one or two descriptions as examples for the learners (see *Procedure*).

Procedure

Class work leading to group or pair work.

Demonstrate the game yourself. Think of an object which may be in the room, or in a picture on the wall, and describe it. Tell the learners to raise their hands if they think they know what you are describing. Finally, see who has guessed correctly.

Then tell everyone to prepare a description in writing of any object; this might be done for homework.

It may help to write down on the board examples of the language items the learners will need, e.g.

It's . . . (colour)
It's . . . (size)
It's . . . (shape)
It's made of . . . (substance)
It's used for . . . (purpose)
It belongs to . . . (owner)

For beginners, you might restrict the choice to common objects. For intermediate and advanced students more bizarre objects, or actions or abstract concepts might be chosen.

Miscellaneous games

96 Fortune-teller

Language	Asking questions with *Who . . .?* and *What . . .?* Reading prepared sentences containing reference to the future with *will*.
Skills	All.
Control	Guided.
Level	Beginners.
Time	30–40 minutes.
Materials	A 'fortune-teller' (see *Preparation*).

Preparation

This device, folded in paper, is known to children in many countries. If you are not sure how it is made, ask some children aged nine or ten.

Have one of these ready before the class begins. Names and numbers are usually written on the outside surfaces. On the inside eight sentences are written, referring to the future.

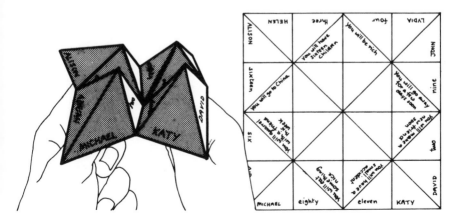

Procedure

Class work leading to pair work.

Show the class your fortune-teller and tell one or two fortunes. The usual exchange between English children is as follows:

A: Who do you love? (*Referring to one of the names on the fortune-teller.*)

B: Michael.

A: M-I-C-H-A-E-L (*Opens and shuts the device as he/she says the letters.*) What number do you want?

B: 8.

A: 1, 2, 3, 4, 5, 6, 7, 8 (*Opens and shuts the device as he/she says the numbers.*) What number do you want now?

B: 3.

A: (*Opens the flap with the number 3 written on it and reads out the fortune written beneath.*) You will go to China!

On the assumption that at least some people in the class will know how to make the device, ask everyone to prepare eight appropriate original sentences referring to the future, e.g.

You will go to China.
You will have 16 children.

Organise the making of the devices so that each learner has one and can write on one side the eight sentences referring to the future and, on the other, names and numbers.

97 Put it together

Language	Reading given texts; putting their component parts in the correct order.
Skills	Reading, and listening in the variation.
Control	Controlled.
Level	Intermediate/advanced.
Time	10–20 minutes; for the variation 20–30 minutes.
Materials	Any appropriate texts; envelopes.

Preparation

Find some short articles in magazines, newspapers or books which will interest your learners. Cut them up into rectangles, cutting between lines, *not* through words. (As the aim is to put the pieces together again you must not cut the pieces in an irregular way because this will help the learners too much!) You may prefer to cut up photocopies of the texts. Interest is added if you choose illustrated articles. Keep each article in a separate envelope. For your own record you might retain a complete photocopy of the article before cutting it up.

The game can be graded in difficulty by (a) the text you choose; (b) the number of pieces you cut the text into; (c) the degree to which pictures help to give the meaning of the text.

Procedure

Pair or individual work.

Give out the envelopes and ask the learners to read each of the pieces and then place them together in the correct order. The learners should ask you to check that the order is correct.

Variation
Group work.

The text here should be a definite story, cut up into strips. A strip is given to each learner in the group, who sit in a circle. Each learner reads out his/her piece of paper, and then they have a general discussion to work out the correct order of the story. They change chairs to sit in the right order and read the whole thing out as the original story.

98   What's in his pocket?

Language	Describing people, actions, etc. on the basis of given evidence, and giving reasons. Degrees of certainty and uncertainty may be expressed.
Skills	Speaking and writing.
Control	Guided.
Level	Advanced.
Time	30–60 minutes.
Materials	A collection of objects; envelopes; paper and pencils.

Preparation

Collect *any* objects which could be carried in someone's pockets, particularly objects collected on a journey or on an evening out. Put a selection of about 15 of the objects in an envelope.

Make up one envelope for each group, or display the 15 objects where everyone can see them.

You can always ask the learners to help you to make a collection of such objects.

Here is an example (it was made at the end of a journey overseas):
1   Air ticket Manchester–Copenhagen–Oslo.
2   Travel agency receipt.
3   Various exchange slips from banks.
4   A small brown paper bag from China.
5   An envelope addressed to Norway with the stamp torn off.
6   A postcard of the mermaid in Copenhagen, stamped but unused.
7   A list of 16 strangely assorted objects.
8   A scrap of paper with 'petrol £5' written on it.
9   Two tickets for an art gallery.
10   A beer mat with a name and number on it.

Procedure

Group work.

The aim of the game is to behave like detectives, trying to understand who the objects belong to, who the person is, what his interests are, where he has been, what he has done, whom he has met, etc.

A full and written account should be made.

The source of the evidence for each claim should be given, e.g.

Mr A. Wright, who lives at 12 Belfield Road, Manchester M20 0BH, bought an air ticket from Delta Travel Agency, Manchester, on 12 July 1983. The ticket was for a flight from Manchester to Oslo via Copenhagen. While he was in Norway he met someone who had been to China (the bag appears to be genuinely from China), etc.

If all groups refer to the same objects, the written accounts may be compared and displayed.

99 What can you do with it?

Language	Explaining the possible uses of objects, e.g. *You can put things in it*, or, more tentatively, *I suppose you could . . .*
Skills	Listening and speaking.
Control	Guided.
Level	Intermediate.
Time	10–15 minutes.
Materials	Chalkboard or OHP; pictures (optional).

Preparation

A list of questions (see *Procedure*). You might like to illustrate these with pictures from magazines. Pictures would stimulate the imagination of the learners but are not essential.

Procedure

Class work.

Write a list of objects on the board or OHP, e.g. a paper bag, a hammer, a pram, an empty tin can, a mirror, a table. Display the pictures if you have them. Ask, e.g.

Teacher: How can you use a paper bag?

Learner 1: You can put things in it.

Teacher: Yes, what else can you do with a paper bag?

Learner 2: You can light a fire with it.
Teacher: Yes. Anything else?
Learner 3: You can blow in it and then make a bang!
Learner 4: You could make it into a ball and throw it at someone to attract their attention!

100   Predicaments

Language	Questions and answers about possible future actions, using the formula *What would do you if. . .? I'd . . .*
Skills	Speaking and listening.
Control	Guided.
Level	Intermediate/advanced.
Time	10–15 minutes.
Materials	None.

Preparation

None.

Procedure

Class work.

One player leaves the room and the others think of a predicament, e.g. running out of petrol in the middle of the country or in a no-parking area in town; the school burning down; losing all one's money.

The player who went out returns and asks the others in turn: 'What would you do if this happened to you?' Each player must give a reasonable answer, in relation to the predicament which has been agreed. The player whose answer finally reveals the predicament to the questioner can go out next.

101 Zip

Language	Calling out numbers according to a given formula.
Skills	Listening and speaking.
Control	Controlled.
Level	Beginners.
Time	5–10 minutes.
Materials	None.

Preparation

None.

Procedure

Class or group work.

The aim of the game is for the learners to count round the class from 1 to 100 without saying a chosen number or a multiple of it. For example, if you and the class choose 4 they must not say 4, 8, 12, 16, 20, etc. Instead of saying one of these numbers the player, whose turn it is, must say 'Zip!', e.g.

Learner 1: One.
Learner 2: Two.
Learner 3: Three.
Learner 4: Zip!
Learner 5: Five.

Summary of the games

Games	Skills	Control	Level	Time in minutes	Organisation	Materials	Prep.	Page
PICTURE GAMES								
1 That's an unusual view!	Listening Speaking	Guided	Beginners	10–15	Class, optional group	Yes	Yes	14
Variation 1	Listening Speaking	Guided	Beginners	10–15	Class, optional group	Yes	Yes	16
Variation 2	Listening Speaking	Guided	Beginners	10–15	Class, optional group	Yes	Yes	16
2 Predicting pictures	Listening Speaking	Guided	Beginners/ intermediate	10–15	Class, group or pair	Yes	Yes	16
3 Happy twins	Listening Speaking	Free	Intermediate	10–15	Pair	Yes	Yes	17
Variation 1	Listening Speaking	Free	All	10–15	Class	Yes	Yes	18
Variation 2	Listening Speaking	Free	All	10–15	Pair	Yes	Yes	18
Variation 3	Listening Speaking Reading	Guided	All	10–15	Pair or group	Yes	Yes	18

4	Describe and draw a picture	Listening Speaking	Free	Intermediate/ advanced	15–20	Pair	Yes	Yes	20
	Variation 1	Listening Speaking	Free	Intermediate/ advanced	15–20	Pair	Yes	Yes	22
	Variation 2	Listening Speaking	Free	Intermediate/ advanced	15–20	Class	Yes	Yes	22
	Variation 3	All	Free	Intermediate/ advanced	20–30	Pair	Yes	Yes	22
	Variation 4	Listening Speaking	Free	Intermediate/ advanced	15–20	Pair or group	Yes	Yes	22
	Variation 5	Listening Speaking	Guided	Beginners	10–15	Class leading to pair	Yes	Yes	22
5	What's the difference?	Listening Speaking	Free	Intermediate/ advanced	5–15	Pair	Yes	Yes	23
	Variation 1	Listening Speaking	Free	Intermediate/ advanced	5–15	Class or pair	Yes	Yes	25
	Variation 2	Listening Speaking	Free	Intermediate/ advanced	15	Pair	Yes	Yes	25
6	Drawing blind	Listening Speaking	Free	Intermediate/ advanced	5–10	Class	Yes	Yes	27
7	Arrange the pictures	Listening Speaking	Free	Intermediate/ advanced	5–15	Pair	Yes	Yes	29
	Variation 1	Listening Speaking	Free	Intermediate/ advanced	5–15	Pair	Yes	Yes	30

Games	Skills	Control	Level	Time in minutes	Organisation	Materials	Prep.	Page
Variation 2	Listening Speaking	Free	Intermediate/ advanced	10–20	Group leading to class	Yes	Yes	30
Variation 3	Listening Speaking	Free	Intermediate/ advanced	10–20	Group as part of class	Yes	Yes	30
Variation 4	Listening Speaking	Free	Intermediate/ advanced	10–20	Pair or group	Yes	Yes	30
Variation 5	Listening Speaking Writing	Free	Intermediate/ advanced	20–30	Group	Yes	Yes	31
Variation 6	Listening Speaking Writing	Free	Intermediate/ advanced	20–30	Class and pair	Yes	Yes	31
Variation 7	Listening Speaking Writing	Free	Intermediate/ advanced	20–30	Class, and pair or individual	Yes	Yes	31
8 Describe and identify the picture	Listening Speaking	Free	Intermediate/ advanced	15–20	Pair	Yes	Yes	32
Variation 1	Listening Speaking Writing	Free	Intermediate/ advanced	15–20	Group	Yes	Yes	32
Variation 2	Listening Speaking Writing	Free	Intermediate/ advanced	15–20	Group	Yes	Yes	33
Variation 3	Listening Speaking	Free	Intermediate/ advanced	15–20	Pair	Yes	Yes	33

No.	Activity	Skills	Control	Level	Time	Grouping			Page
9	Are you a good detective?	All	Guided	Intermediate/advanced	20–40	Class	Yes	Yes	33
	Variation	All	Guided	Intermediate/advanced	20–40	Class	Yes	Yes	34
10	Picture/text matching	Reading (Listening) (Speaking)	Controlled	All	Varies	Individual or pair	Yes	Yes	34
	Variation	All	Guided	All	Varies	Pair or group leading to class	Yes	Yes	36

PSYCHOLOGY GAMES

No.	Activity	Skills	Control	Level	Time	Grouping			Page
11	Telepathy	Listening Speaking	Controlled	Beginners	20–30	Class leading to pair	Yes	Yes	37
	Variation	Listening Speaking Reading	Controlled	Beginners	10–15	Class	Yes	Yes	38
12	Visual perception of length	Listening Speaking	Guided	Beginners	22–23	Class leading to pair	Yes	Yes	39
	Variation 1	All	Guided	Beginners	5–10	Pair	Yes	Yes	41
	Variation 2	All	Guided	Beginners	5–10	Pair	Yes	Yes	41
	Variation 3	All	Guided	Beginners	5–10	Pair	Yes	Yes	42
	Variation 4	All	Guided	Beginners	5–10	Pair	Yes	Yes	42
	Variation 5	All	Guided	Beginners	5–10	Pair	Yes	Yes	42

Games	Skills	Control	Level	Time in minutes	Organisation	Materials	Prep.	Page
13 The old woman and the young woman	Listening Speaking	Guided	Beginners	22–23	Class leading to pair	Yes	Yes	43
14 Blobs	Listening Speaking	Guided	Beginners/intermediate	10–15 (+10–15)	Class leading to pair	Yes	Yes	45
Variation	Listening Speaking	Free	Advanced	Varies	Class	Yes	Yes	46
15 How quickly can you see?	Listening Speaking	Guided	All	5–10	Class leading to pair	Yes	Yes	46
16 Faces and character	Listening Speaking	Free	Intermediate/advanced	5	Class leading to pair	Yes	Yes	48
17 Visual imagery	Speaking Writing	Free	Advanced	5–10	Class	None	None	49
Variation 1	Listening Speaking	Free	Advanced	10–20	Class or pair	None	None	49
Variation 2	Listening Speaking	Free	Advanced	10–20	Class	None	None	50
Variation 3	Writing	Free	Advanced	10–20	Class	Yes	None	50
18 Palmistry	Listening Speaking	Free	Advanced	30–60	Class, optional pair or individual	Yes	Yes	51
19 A memory system	Listening Speaking Writing	Guided	Intermediate/advanced	20–30	Class leading to pair	Yes	Yes	54

Games	Skills	Control	Level	Time in minutes	Organisation	Materials	Prep.	Page
28 Getting to know each other	All	Guided	All	15–20	Class	Yes	Yes	71
Variation	All	Guided	All	15–20	Class	Yes	Yes	72
29 Guess who it is	Listening Speaking	Guided	Intermediate/advanced	30–40	Class or group	Yes	None	73
Variation	Listening Speaking	Guided	Intermediate/advanced	30–40	Group	None	None	73
30 Truth, dare and promise	All	Guided	Beginners/intermediate	20–30	Individual leading to group	Yes	Yes	74
31 Six eyes	All	Guided	Intermediate/advanced	30	Group	Yes	None	75
32 Questionnaires	All	Guided	All	20–30	Pair leading to group or class	Yes	Yes	76
Variation 1	All	Guided	All	20–30	Group or class	Yes	Yes	76
Variation 2	All	Guided	All	20–30	Pair	Yes	Yes	77
Variation 3	All	Guided	All	20–30	Pair	Yes	Yes	77
33 Fortune-telling	All	Free	All	30	Group	Yes	None	77
34 Personal opinions	All	Free	All	30	Group or class	Yes	None	78
35 Reading someone's mind	Listening Speaking	Free	Intermediate/advanced	10–15	Class	None	None	80

CARD AND BOARD GAMES

36 **Snakes and ladders**	Speaking Reading	Controlled	Beginners	Varies	Pair or group	Yes	Yes	81
Variation 1	Speaking Reading	Controlled	Beginners/ intermediate	Varies	Pair or group	Yes	Yes	82
Variation 2	Speaking Reading Writing	Guided or free	Beginners/ intermediate	Varies	Pair or group	Yes	Yes	83
37 **Happy families**	Listening Speaking	Controlled	Beginners/ intermediate	5	Group	Yes	Yes	83
Variation	Listening Speaking Reading	Controlled	Beginners/ intermediate	5	Group	Yes	Yes	84
38 **Search**	All	Controlled or guided	Intermediate	15	Pair	Yes	Yes	85
Variation	All	Guided or free	Intermediate	20–30	Pair	Yes	Yes	88
39 **Presents, and rewards and punishments**	Listening Speaking	Free	Advanced	20	Group	Yes	Yes	88
Variation 1	Listening Speaking	Free	Advanced	20	Group	Yes	Yes	89
Variation 2	All	Free	Advanced	25	Group	Yes	Yes	90
Variation 3	Listening Speaking	Free	Advanced	20	Group	Yes	Yes	90

Games	Skills	Control	Level	Time in minutes	Organisation	Materials	Prep.	Page
SOUND GAMES								
40 Voices and objects	Listening Speaking	Guided	Beginners	5–10	Class	Yes	None	91
41 Actions by one person	Listening Speaking	Guided	Beginners	10–15	Class	None	Yes	92
42 Listening to sounds	Listening Speaking	Guided	Beginners/intermediate	5–10	Class	None	None	93
43 Actions by two people or more	Listening Speaking	Guided	Intermediate	10–15	Class	Yes	Yes	94
44 Using the tape recorder	Listening Speaking	Guided	Intermediate/advanced	20–30	Class or group	Yes	Yes	96
STORY GAMES								
45 Guess what I'm drawing	Listening Speaking	Guided	Beginners	15–25	Class, optional pair	Yes	None	98
46 Silly stories	Listening Speaking	Free	Intermediate/advanced	5–10	Class	None	None	99
47 Fantasy stories	All	Free	Intermediate/advanced	30	Group or pair, leading to class	Yes	Yes	100
Variation 1	All	Free	Intermediate/advanced	30	Group or pair, leading to class	Yes	Yes	100

	Skills	Guided/Free	Level	Number	Grouping			Page
Variation 2	All	Free	Intermediate/advanced	30	Group leading to class	Yes	Yes	101
Variation 3	Listening Speaking	Free	Intermediate/advanced	Varies	Group	Yes	Yes	101
Variation 4	All	Free	Intermediate/advanced	Varies	Individual or pair, leading to class	None	None	101
Variation 5	Listening Speaking	Free	Intermediate/advanced	Varies	Group	Yes	Yes	101
48 Build a story	Listening Speaking	Guided	Intermediate/advanced	20	Class	Yes	Yes	102
49 Confabulation, or the key sentence	All	Free	Advanced	30–40	Group or pair, leading to class	None	Yes	104
50 Consequences	All	Guided	Intermediate	10	Group leading to class	Yes	None	105
Variation	All	Guided	Intermediate	10	Group leading to class	Yes	None	106
51 Bits and pieces	Listening Speaking Writing	Guided/free	All	15–40	Group	Yes	Yes	107
Variation 1	Listening	Guided/free	All	15–40	Group leading to class	Yes	Yes	107
Variation 2	Listening Speaking Reading	Guided/free	All	15–40	Group	Yes	Yes	107
Variation 3	Listening Speaking Reading	Guided/free	All	15–40	Class	Yes	Yes	107

Games	Skills	Control	Level	Time in minutes	Organisation	Materials	Prep.	Page
Variation 4	Listening Speaking Reading	Guided/free	All	15–40	Group	Yes	Yes	107
Variation 5	Listening Speaking Reading	Guided/free	All	15–40	Group	Yes	Yes	107
Variation 6	Listening Speaking Reading	Guided/free	All	15–40	Group or class	Yes	Yes	108
52 Domino story	Listening Speaking	Free	All	20	Group	Yes	Yes	109
53 Change the story	All	Free	Intermediate/advanced	30–40	Group	Yes	None	110
54 Leonardo's strip!	All	Free	All	30	Individual or pair	Yes	Yes	111

WORD GAMES

Games	Skills	Control	Level	Time in minutes	Organisation	Materials	Prep.	Page
55 Bingo	All	Controlled	Beginners	10–20	Class	Yes	Yes	113
Variation 1	All	Controlled	Beginners	10–20	Class	Yes	Yes	114
Variation 2	All	Controlled	Beginners/intermediate	10–20	Class	Yes	Yes	114
Variation 3	All	Controlled	Beginners/intermediate	10–20	Class	Yes	Yes	115

	Name	Skills	Control	Level	Number	Organization			Page
56	Dash it and hang it	All	Guided	Beginners/intermediate	2–3	Class	Yes	None	115
	Variation 1	All	Guided	Beginners/intermediate	2–3	Class or pair	Yes	None	116
	Variation 2	All	Guided	Beginners/intermediate	2–3	Class or pair	Yes	None	117
57	A–A, B–B	Listening Speaking Writing	Guided	Beginners/intermediate	15	Group leading to team	Yes	Yes	118
	Variation	Listening Speaking	Guided	Beginners/intermediate	5–10	Group or class	None	Yes	119
58	Make a sentence	All	Guided	Beginners/intermediate	35	Individual leading to class or group	Yes	Yes	120
	Variation	All	Controlled	Beginners/intermediate	20–25	Class leading to group	Yes	Yes	121
59	The odd man out	All	Guided	Intermediate	10	Class	Yes	Yes	122
	Variation	All	Guided	Advanced	10	Group or pair	Yes	Yes	123
60	Connections	Listening Speaking	Guided	Intermediate/advanced	5–10	Class, group or pair	None	None	124
	Variation 1	Listening Speaking	Guided	Intermediate/advanced	5–10	Class or group	Yes	Yes	125
	Variation 2	Listening Speaking	Guided	Intermediate/advanced	5–10	Class or group	Yes	Yes	125
	Variation 3	Listening Speaking	Free	Intermediate/advanced	30	Group	Yes	Yes	125

Games	Skills	Control	Level	Time in minutes	Organisation	Materials	Prep.	Page
Variation 4	Listening Speaking Reading	Free	Intermediate/ advanced	30	Class	Yes	Yes	126
61 Missing words	All	Guided	Intermediate/ advanced	Varies	Pair	Yes	Yes	126
62 Additions	Listening Speaking Writing	Guided	Intermediate/ advanced	5	Group leading to class	Yes	None	127
63 Definitions	Listening Speaking	Guided	Advanced	10–15	Class leading to pair	None	Yes	128
64 Daft definitions	All	Guided	Advanced	10–20	Individual or group, leading to class	Yes	Yes	129
65 Deletions	Listening Speaking Reading	Guided	Advanced	10–15	Class	Yes	Yes	130
TRUE/FALSE GAMES								
66 Repeat it if it's true	Listening Speaking	Controlled	Beginners	5–10	Class	Yes	Yes	133
67 Correct me if I'm wrong	Listening Speaking Reading	Guided	All	10	Class, group or pair	Yes	Yes	134

No.	Name	Skills	Control	Level	Number	Grouping	Prep.	Prep.	Page
68	Don't let them pull your leg	Listening Speaking Writing	Free	All	18–24	Class, group or pair	None	None	135
69	Super sleuth	Listening Speaking Reading	Guided	Intermediate/ advanced	20–30	Class	Yes	Yes	136
70	There's something wrong somewhere	Reading	Guided	All	Varies	Class or group	Yes	Yes	137
71	One of them isn't telling the truth	Listening	Free	All	22–23	Pair leading to class or group	Yes	Yes	138

MEMORY GAMES

No.	Name	Skills	Control	Level	Number	Grouping	Prep.	Prep.	Page
72	What's behind you?	Listening Speaking	Free	Beginners/ intermediate	2–3	Class	None	None	139
	Variation 1	Listening Speaking Reading	Free	Beginners/ intermediate	5	Class	None	None	140
	Variation 2	Listening Speaking	Free	Beginners/ intermediate	2–3	Pair	None	None	140
73	Kim's game	Listening Speaking Writing	Guided	Beginners/ intermediate	5	Class leading to optional pair	Yes	Yes	140
	Variation 1	Listening Speaking Writing	Guided	Beginners/ intermediate	5	Class	Yes	Yes	141

Games	Skills	Control	Level	Time in minutes	Organisation	Materials	Prep.	Page
Variation 2	Listening Speaking Writing	Guided	Beginners/intermediate	5	Class	Yes	Yes	141
Variation 3	Listening Speaking Writing	Guided	Beginners/intermediate	5	Class	Yes	Yes	142
Variation 4	Listening Speaking Writing	Guided	Beginners/intermediate	5	Class	Yes	Yes	142
Variation 5	Listening Speaking Writing	Guided	Beginners/intermediate	5	Class leading to pair	Yes	Yes	142
Variation 6	All	Guided	Advanced	20–30	Individual leading to pair	Yes	Yes	143
Variation 7	Listening Speaking Writing	Free	Advanced	20–30	Group	Yes	Yes	143
74 Pass the message	All	Controlled or free	All	10–15	Class	Yes	Yes	144
Variation 1	All	Controlled or free	All	10–15	Class	None	Yes	145
Variation 2	All	Controlled	All	10–15	Class	None	Yes	145
Variation 3	All	Controlled or free	All	Varies	Class	None	Yes	145

75	Pass the picture	Listening Speaking	Free	Intermediate/advanced	10–15	Class	Yes	Yes	146
76	Pelmanism	Listening Speaking Reading	Guided	All	10–15	Group	Yes	Yes	147
	Variation 1	Reading (*or* Listening Speaking Reading)	Guided	All	10–15	Individual or pair	Yes	Yes	148
	Variation 2	Listening Speaking Reading	Guided	Beginners/intermediate	5–10	Group	Yes	Yes	149
77	Would you make a good witness?	Listening Speaking	Free	Intermediate/advanced	10–15	Class	Yes	Yes	149
	Variation 1	All	Free	Intermediate/advanced	20	Class and group	Yes	Yes	150
	Variation 2	Listening Speaking	Free	Intermediate/advanced	5–10	Class	Yes	Yes	150
	Variation 3	Listening Speaking	Free	Intermediate/advanced	5–10	Class	Yes	Yes	151

QUESTION AND ANSWER GAMES

78	Don't say 'Yes' or 'No'	Listening Speaking	Guided	Intermediate/advanced	5–10	Class leading to group or pair	None	None	152

Games	Skills	Control	Level	Time in minutes	Organisation	Materials	Prep.	Page
79 Half the class knows	Listening Speaking	Free	All	5–10	Class leading to group or pair	Yes	Yes	153
80 Test your knowledge	Reading	Controlled	Intermediate/ advanced	10–20	Individual or pair	Yes	Yes	155
Variation	Reading	Controlled	Intermediate/ advanced	10–20	Individual or pair	Yes	Yes	157
81 Twenty questions	Listening Speaking	Free	Intermediate/ advanced	15	Class	None	None	157
Variation 1	Listening Speaking	Free	Intermediate/ advanced	15	Class	None	Yes	158
Variation 2	Listening Speaking	Free	Intermediate/ advanced	15	Class	None	None	158
Variation 3	Listening Speaking	Free	Intermediate/ advanced	15	Class	None	None	158
Variation 4	Listening Speaking	Free	Intermediate/ advanced	15	Class	None	None	158
Variation 5	Listening Speaking	Free	Intermediate/ advanced	15	Group or class	None	None	158
82 General knowledge quiz	Listening Speaking	Free	Intermediate/ advanced	10–15	Class	None	Yes	159
83 What were you doing last night?	Listening Speaking	Free	Intermediate/ advanced	10–15	Class	None	None	161

	Skills	Type	Level	Time	Grouping			Page
84 Who are you?	All	Free	Intermediate/advanced	60–80	Individual leading to class and pair	Yes	Yes	162
Variation	Listening Speaking	Free	Intermediate/advanced	5	Group	Yes	Yes	163
85 Flipping	Listening Speaking	Free	Intermediate/advanced	5	Class and group	None	None	163
86 Avoidance	Listening Speaking	Free	Intermediate/advanced	5	Class and group	None	None	164
87 Alibis	Listening Speaking	Free	Intermediate/advanced	40–45	Pair leading to class	None	None	165
Variation	Listening Speaking	Guided	Beginners/intermediate	10	Group	Yes	Yes	166
88 Distractions	Listening Speaking	Free	All	2–3	Class or group	Yes	None	167
Variation	Listening Speaking	Free	All	2–3	Class or group	Yes	None	167
89 Questions for answers	All	Guided	All	10	Individual or pair, leading to class	Yes	Yes	168
Variation	Listening Speaking Reading	Guided	All	10	Class	Yes	Yes	168

GUESSING AND SPECULATING GAMES

	Skills	Type	Level	Time	Grouping			Page
90 Hiding and finding	Listening Speaking	Guided	Beginners	15	Class	Yes	None	169

Games	Skills	Control	Level	Time in minutes	Organisation	Materials	Prep.	Page
Variation 1	Listening Speaking	Guided	Intermediate	15	Class	Yes	None	170
Variation 2	Listening Speaking	Guided	Intermediate	15	Class	Yes	None	170
91 **Feel and think**	Listening Speaking	Guided	Beginners/ intermediate	12–13	Class, leading to optional pair	Yes	Yes	171
Variation 1	Listening Speaking	Guided	Advanced	10	Class, leading to optional pair	Yes	Yes	172
Variation 2	Listening Speaking	Guided	Beginners/ intermediate	10	Group or class	Yes	Yes	172
92 **One idea at a time**	Listening Speaking	Guided	Beginners/ intermediate	10–15	Class	None	None	173
Variation 1	Listening Speaking	Guided	Beginners/ intermediate	10–15	Class	None	None	174
Variation 2	Listening Speaking	Guided	Beginners/ intermediate	10–15	Class	None	None	174
Variation 3	Listening Speaking	Guided	Beginners/ intermediate	10–15	Class	None	None	174
Variation 4	Listening Speaking	Guided	Beginners/ intermediate	10–15	Class	None	None	174
93 **Picture out of focus**	Listening Speaking	Free	Intermediate/ advanced	10–15	Class	Yes	Yes	175

94 **Box**	Listening Speaking	Free	All	5	Class	Yes	Yes	176
Variation	Listening Speaking	Free	All	5	Class	Yes	Yes	177
95 **What on earth is he talking about?**	All	Free	All	15–30	Class, leading to group or pair	None	Yes	177

MISCELLANEOUS GAMES

96 **Fortune-teller**	All	Guided	Beginners	30–40	Class leading to pair	Yes	Yes	179
97 **Put it together**	Reading	Controlled	Intermediate/ advanced	10–20	Pair or individual	Yes	Yes	181
Variation	Listening Speaking Reading	Controlled	Intermediate/ advanced	20–30	Group	Yes	Yes	181
98 **What's in his pocket?**	Speaking Writing	Guided	Advanced	30–60	Group	Yes	Yes	182
99 **What can you do with it?**	Listening Speaking	Guided	Intermediate	10–15	Class	Yes	Yes	183
100 **Predicaments**	Listening Speaking	Guided	Intermediate/ advanced	10–15	Class	None	None	184
101 **Zip**	Listening Speaking	Controlled	Beginners	5–10	Class or group	None	None	185

Index

Structures

Only the major structural items and their principal occurrences are listed here. The numbers given below refer to the games, *not* the pages. See also pp. 8–13, where *Language for the organisation of games* is outlined.

ADJECTIVES

colours 12, 26, 57, 59, 73
comparison (*too . . ., -er than*, etc.) 4, 5, 6, 9, 12, 73 (Var. 5 and Var. 6), 75
personal characteristics 10(Var.), 13, 16, 18, 28, 29, 32, 34, 35, 39(Var.), 77, 84, 92, 98
size 12
various 26, 55(Var. 3), 57, 58, 59, 64, 73(Var. 2), 91 (Var. 1), 94, 95

ADVERBS

degree 35
manner 92(Var. 1)
time 31
various 55(Var. 3), 57, 58, 64

CONJUNCTIONS

cause/reason (*because*, etc.) 59, 60, 98
condition (*if*) 32(Var. 1), 50, 100
result (*so*) 50
various 48, 52, 55, (Var. 3), 57, 58

DETERMINERS

cardinal numerals (*one, two*, etc.) 24, 36, 55, 73(Var. 1), 101
possessives (*my, your* etc.) 94
quantifiers (*all, any, some*, etc.) 21, 72
various 55(Var. 3), 57, 58

NOUNS

genitive (*'s* and *s'*) 12, 26, 94
jobs 92(Var. 2)
objects 1, 2, 3, 4, 5, 6, 7, 8, 14, 15, 17, 19, 26, 29, 37, 39, 40, 45, 57, 70, 71, 72, 73, 91, 94, 98, 99

Types of communication

Only the major types of communication (often called language functions) and their principal occurrences are listed here. The numbers given below refer to the games, *not* the pages. See also pp. 8–13, where *Language for the organisation of games* is outlined.

STATING FACTS

naming and identifying things, people and actions 1, 2, 8, 10, 13, 14, 19, 21, 25, 26, 27, 29, 31, 32, 40, 45, 55, 57, 59, 70, 71, 72, 73, 91, 94, 95
describing things, people and actions 1, 3, 4, 5, 7, 8, 9, 10, 11, 14, 15, 16, 17, 18, 28, 29, 30, 31, 34, 35, 38, 39, 45, 48, 51, 55(Var. 2), 63, 64, 66, 69, 71, 72, 73, 75, 76, 77, 92, 93, 94, 95, 98, 99
comparing things 4, 5, 6, 9, 12, 61, 64, 69, 70, 73(Var. 5 and Var. 6), 75
narrating and reporting (past events) 15, 20, 43, 44, 46, 47, 48, 49, 50, 51, 52, 53, 54, 77, 83, 87
commentating (present events) 17, 21, 22, 23, 41, 42, 44, 73(Var. 4), 92(Var. 3)
predicting (future events) 2, 18, 20, 22, 23, 33, 96, 100

STATING OPINIONS AND FEELINGS

agreement and disagreement 39, 59, 62, 64, 65, 76, 82
doubt 82, 91, 93, 98
ignorance 1, 82
personal attitudes 28, 29, 30, 31, 32, 34, 35, 39, 84
pleasure 2, 18
praise and encouragement 4, 6, 7
regret 2, 18
speculation 12, 16, 45, 51, 56, 82, 90, 93
surprise 13, 18
sympathy 18

ASKING QUESTIONS

questions of fact 4, 5, 7, 8(Var. 3), 11, 21, 25, 26, 30, 32, 38, 40, 45, 51, 63, 78, 79, 80, 81, 82, 83, 84, 85, 86, 87, 88, 89, 90, 91, 92, 96
questions about others' opinions and feelings 28, 30, 32, 84, 86, 88, 89, 92, 96

OTHER USES OF LANGUAGE

challenges 30
correcting and criticising 4, 6, 9, 67, 68, 69, 70, 71
orders and instructions 6, 7, 24, 30, 36, 48, 92
promising 30, 50
reasons 59, 60, 98

Alphabetical list of games

The first number, in bold type, refers to the game, the second number to the page.

418.007
W947

LINCOLN CHRISTIAN COLLEGE AND SEMINARY 87242

418.007 Wright, Andrew,
W947   Games for
           language learning

                        87242

DEMCO